Access Granted

Mastering Strategic Meetings and Events

By
Blessing Enakimio

"ACCESS IS THE MOST POWERFUL ASSET - ONE THAT EMPOWERS CONNECTIONS, FOSTERS PARTNERSHIPS AND IGNITES GLOBAL POSSIBILITIES."

DR. BLESSING ENAKIMIO

Foreword

The intersection of strategic management and events is now more critical than ever in today's evolving business landscape. Business leaders are constantly faced with the challenges that require not only foresight and planning, but adaptability and innovation. Dr Blessing in this book has managed to identify and cover the critical aspects of how strategic event planning can help in transforming business challenges into real opportunities.

Using her extensive experience, Dr Blessing has managed through a diverse array of insights and practical case studies to demonstrate the power of strategic management. Her ability to delve into the intricate relationship between strategy and planning and the planning and execution of events – be they corporate conferences, product launches, or community engagements – reflect a wider understanding of how to align events within the framework of business objectives.

As a reader of this book, you will embark on a journey of discovery of new ideas and practical tools that you will be able to incorporate into your event planning strategy. As somebody who has worked closely with Dr Blessing on a number of international events over a number of years, I'm excited to see so much of the experience being put into practical book for others to use.

Paul Mervin

My name is **Bolaji Sofoluwe**, and I have been privileged to be connected to Blessing Enakimio for a couple of years now. In that time, I've had the opportunity to witness first-hand the brilliance, passion, and commitment that Blessing brings to her work. Events have an extraordinary way of bringing people together for good, but this happens only when they are executed with purpose and intention. This book is timely, necessary, and could not have been written by anyone more qualified than Blessing, a visionary who has meticulously curated and organised countless strategic meetings and events on both local and international stages.

As a business leader in international trade and business growth, I cannot over-emphasise the significance of well-structured, impactful meetings and events. I've attended many events over the years, and I have seen the full spectrum—some events have been highly impactful, while others have left much to be desired. Poorly organised events can lead to lost opportunities, waste precious time, and frustrate participants. I have also witnessed the magic of well-planned events, which can be transformative, fostering new ideas, generating meaningful collaborations, and unlocking new potential for businesses and individuals that attend. The difference is most likely, in the details, the strategy, and the vision that goes into the planning. These are the elements that Blessing has mastered, and that she will generously share in this book.

Blessing's experience speaks volumes. Having organised some of the largest events in the West African region, her work has brought together key stakeholders and players from around the globe. She has facilitated discussions that have shaped industries and policies and created opportunities for partnerships beyond borders. I have personally observed her work with the Nigeria International Energy Summit.

"Access Granted" is more than just a guide—it is an invitation to level up. Whether you are a seasoned event planner, a business leader, or someone who simply wants to understand how to make meetings and events more productive, this book is a resource you will return to again and again.

I strongly believe we are at the start of a revolution in events - they have become the cornerstone of many industries. This book will serve as both a blueprint and a source of inspiration.

I highly recommend this book to anyone who wishes to master the art and science of strategic events. Blessing Enakimio has proven time and time again that she is a thought leader in this space, and her insights are bound to transform the way you approach your next event. Her work has already impacted countless businesses and individuals, and I have no doubt that the wisdom contained in ***"Access Granted"*** will do the same for you.

My name is **Dr. Isaac Enakimio**, and it's an honour to write this foreword for *Access Granted: Mastering Strategic Meetings and Events*. Watching my incredible wife excel in the world of events management has been a constant source of inspiration. From her early days delivering corporate events at Ofsted, she didn't just organise sessions - she created transformative moments that brought people together, fostering collaboration and growth in ways others might overlook.

Over the years, she has mastered the art of turning events into strategic tools for success, building access for companies to seize new opportunities and forge lasting connections. Her ability to plan with purpose, beyond aesthetics, is what sets her apart. She crafts every event with the same care and precision, always aligning them with broader business goals to create meaningful impact.

What inspires me most is her resilience and grace in an industry that often presents challenges. Navigating a male-dominated space, she faces biases head-on, but she lets her work speak for itself - always delivering results with professionalism and brilliance. Her events go beyond the aesthetic; they are strategic, purposeful and designed to deliver results long after the event has ended.

This book, *Access Granted*, is a reflection of everything she has achieved and stands as a blueprint for transforming meetings and events into opportunities for growth and success. It's not just a guide; it's a resource for anyone who wants to understand how events can unlock access to something greater.

To my brilliant wife, thank you for inspiring me and so many others. Your dedication, creativity, and unwavering talent continue to shine through, and I couldn't be prouder of the difference you make in the lives of so many.

Contents

Introduction: The Power of Connection

Every significant achievement in my career has been built on one fundamental truth: it's all about people. From the grandest global summits to the most intimate networking dinners, the common thread that weaves through every successful event is the power of human connection. This book is born out of my ultimate purpose; to facilitate those connections on a global scale, turning moments into movements and gatherings into gateways for opportunity.

My journey in the world of events and meetings has spanned decades, continents and industries, yet the essence of what I do remains unchanged: bringing people together in meaningful ways. This book is a reflection of that journey, packed with the lessons learned from years of navigating the intricate dynamics of event management, corporate strategy and economic development. But more than that, it's a guide for you, whether you are an event organiser or a participant, to harness the power of connection for your own success.

Why This Book?

In a world where digital communication often reigns supreme, the tangible, face-to-face interactions that events facilitate have never been more valuable. Whether you're closing a business deal, forging a new partnership, or simply expanding your network, the environment in which you connect matters. This book is your essential guide to maximising your impact and value in the events industry, giving you the tools to navigate this dynamic landscape with confidence and purpose.

I've seen first-hand how a well-crafted event can be a catalyst for transformation, both for individuals and for entire organisations. Events are where ideas are exchanged, innovations are born and relationships are solidified. They are where opportunities are created, deals are made and ultimately, where business gets done. And it's not just about the immediate outcomes; it's about the ripple effects that extend far beyond the event itself, shaping the future in ways that are often unexpected yet profoundly impactful.

The Strategic Advantage

Throughout this book, you'll find a blend of strategic insight, practical advice and a bit of fun too. Because while the work we do in this industry is serious business, it's also deeply rewarding and sometimes, it's just plain enjoyable. We'll explore how to leverage events to gain a competitive edge, from designing experiences that resonate with your audience to strategically attending events that align with your professional goals.

One of the guiding principles of my work and something you'll see reflected in these pages is my alignment with Sustainable Development Goal 17 (SDG17): Partnerships for the Goals. Collaboration is at the heart of progress and events are the perfect platforms to foster the partnerships that drive real change. Whether you're working on a local or global scale, the power of collective action cannot be overstated.

The Meeting Economy

This brings us to a concept I hold close - the Meeting Economy. Events are more than just gatherings; they are vital economic engines that drive industries, create jobs and stimulate growth. The Meeting Economy captures the essence of this phenomenon, highlighting the significant role that meetings, conferences and events play in local and global economies. It's about understanding that every handshake, every conversation and every connection has the potential to open doors, spark innovation and transform lives.

Ultimately, it's all about People.

But ultimately, it's all about people. That's what this book is really about, how we can come together, connect and create something bigger than ourselves. It's about understanding that every handshake, every conversation and every connection has the potential to open doors, spark innovation and transform lives.

So, whether you're an organiser looking to craft unforgettable experiences or a participant eager to make the most of your time at the next big conference, this book is for you. It's a strategic guide, an educational resource and yes, even a bit of fun along the way. Because when it comes to the world of meetings and events, the journey is just as important as the destination.

Welcome to *Access Granted: Mastering Strategic Meetings and Events.*

Let's connect.

Part I: The Event Organiser's Playbook

Chapter 1: Event Strategy and Design

When it comes to events, success does not happen by accident. It is the result of careful planning, strategic thinking and a deep understanding of what makes an experience memorable. Event strategy and design are the foundation upon which every successful event is built. Without a clear vision and thoughtful execution, even the most well-funded events can fall flat. In this chapter, we will explore the art and science of crafting events that not only meet objectives but also resonate deeply with attendees.

Understanding the Event Lifecycle

Imagine planning an event as embarking on a journey. Every successful event unfolds through a series of stages, each one building on the last. This journey is known as the event lifecycle, a roadmap that guides you from the initial spark of an idea to the final reflections after the event concludes. Understanding this lifecycle is crucial for navigating each phase with confidence and clarity.

The journey begins with **conception and vision**. Every event starts as an idea - a vision of what could be. This is the stage where you define the purpose of the event. What do you want to achieve? How do you want attendees to feel when they walk away? What impact should this event have on your brand, your business, or the broader industry? These are not just questions; they are the pillars upon which your entire event will rest. A clear, compelling vision sets the tone for everything that follows.

Once your vision is in place, you move into **planning and development**. This is where the idea begins to take shape. You assemble the right team, set a budget and develop a timeline. It is a stage filled with choices selecting a venue, curating speakers, designing the agenda. Every decision should align with the overarching goals of the event. But it is not just about logistics; it is about creating a framework that will bring your vision to life. This is where the event starts to feel real, where abstract ideas are translated into concrete plans.

Then comes **execution and experience** - the moment of truth. This is when all your planning is put to the test. The lights go up, the doors open and your vision becomes reality. During this phase, every detail matters. From the lighting in the venue to the flow of the agenda, everything plays a role in shaping the attendee experience. This is also where your ability to adapt is crucial. No matter how well you plan, there will always be surprises. The key is to handle them with grace, ensuring that the experience remains seamless for your attendees.

Finally, the journey concludes with **post-event evaluation**. But while the event itself may be over; the work is not. This phase is about reflection, taking the time to assess what worked, what did not and what could be improved. It involves gathering feedback from attendees, conducting debriefs with your team and analysing key performance indicators (KPIs). The goal is not just to evaluate this event but to learn from it, to ensure that each event you plan is better than the last. This is where the seeds for your next event are planted, ensuring that the cycle of improvement continues.

Design Thinking for Events

Design thinking is a powerful approach to creating events that are not only effective but also memorable. It is about putting the attendee at the centre of your planning process, ensuring that every aspect of the event is designed with their needs and expectations in mind.

Imagine stepping into the shoes of your attendees. What do they see? What do they feel? What do they need? This is where the process of **empathising with your audience** begins. Understanding your audience is the first step in design thinking. Who are they? What are their pain points? What motivates them to attend your event? By putting yourself in their shoes, you can design an experience that speaks directly to their needs and aspirations.

Once you have a clear understanding of your audience, the next step is to **define your event's value proposition**. What unique value does your event offer? Whether it is access to exclusive insights, unparalleled networking opportunities, or a chance to experience something new, your event's value proposition should be clear and compelling. This value proposition will guide every decision you make, from the content of your sessions to the choice of venue.

With a clear value proposition in mind, it is time to **ideate and innovate**. This is where creativity comes into play. Do not be afraid to think outside the box. The best events often come from bold ideas and innovative approaches. Brainstorm with your team, consider what has not been done before and explore new ways to engage your audience. This is where the seeds of a truly memorable event are planted.

But before you commit fully to your ideas, it is important to **prototype and test** them. This could involve creating mock agendas, conducting focus groups, or running pilot sessions. Testing your ideas on a small scale allows you to refine them, ensuring they resonate with your audience and achieve the desired impact. This iterative process is key to ensuring that your event delivers on its promises.

Finally, with your design solidified, it is time to **implement and refine**. But remember, design thinking is not a one-time process, it is iterative. Be prepared to refine your approach based on real-time feedback during the event. This agility can be the difference between an event that meets expectations and one that exceeds them.

The Art of Curation

Curation is an often-overlooked aspect of event strategy, but it is one of the most critical. A well-curated event delivers value by aligning every element; from speakers and sessions to themes and formats, with the strategic goals you have set.

Think of curation as crafting a narrative for your event. Your **speaker selection** is the voice of that narrative. Speakers are the heart of your event. They should not only be experts in their fields but also capable of engaging and inspiring your audience. It is not just about star power; it is about relevance and resonance. Choose speakers who align with your event's goals and who can provide the insights or inspiration that your attendees seek.

But a great narrative is more than just its characters, it is also about **thematic coherence**. Every element of your event should be connected by a common theme or message. This coherence helps to reinforce your event's objectives and ensures that attendees leave with a clear understanding of the key takeaways. Whether it is sustainability, innovation, or industry disruption, your theme should be woven through the content, branding and even the atmosphere of the event.

As you build your narrative, consider the **format and flow** of your event. The structure of your event; the mix of keynotes, panels, workshops and networking opportunities should be carefully curated to maximise engagement and value. Consider the flow of the day: when should the most intensive sessions occur? When is it time for a break or a networking opportunity? The right format can enhance learning, foster connections and keep your audience energised throughout the event.

Finally, think about **content curation**. Beyond choosing the right speakers, curating the content itself is crucial. What topics will resonate most with your audience? How can you ensure a balance between depth and breadth? Content should be relevant, actionable and aligned with the broader goals of your event. It should challenge your audience, spark new ideas and provide real value that they can take away.

Chapter Summary

Event strategy and design is about intentionality. It is about making deliberate choices at every stage of the event lifecycle to create experiences that are not only effective but also memorable. By understanding the lifecycle of an event, applying design thinking principles and mastering the art of curation, you can craft events that resonate deeply with your audience and achieve your strategic goals.

A well-designed event is more than just a series of activities; it is an experience that moves people, drives business and leaves a lasting impact. As we continue through this book, we will delve deeper into the practicalities of event management, but always with this foundation of strategy and design in mind. This is where every successful event begins and it is the key to ensuring that your events are not just successful but truly unforgettable.

Chapter 2: Crafting a Memorable Experience

Every event is an opportunity to create a lasting impression. Whether it is a conference, a gala, or a small roundtable discussion, the experience you craft for your attendees will define their memories of the event and by extension, their perception of your brand, your organisation and your message. Crafting a memorable experience is both an art and a science, requiring attention to detail, creativity and a deep understanding of what truly resonates with people. In this chapter, we will explore the key elements that contribute to creating an unforgettable event experience, from sensory engagement to storytelling and how these elements can be strategically employed to leave a lasting impact.

The Power of First Impressions

First impressions matter and in the context of an event, they are formed long before the attendees step through the doors. The experience begins with the very first touchpoint whether it is the invitation, the registration process, or the pre-event communications. Each of these elements sets the tone and builds anticipation, shaping the expectations of your attendees.

Consider the invitation. Is it simply a functional piece of communication, or does it reflect the essence of the event? A well-designed invitation, whether digital or printed, can evoke curiosity, excitement and a sense of exclusivity. It is the first opportunity to communicate your event's theme, purpose and style. The language, design and even the medium you choose all contribute to the impression you are creating. A generic, uninspired invitation might lead to lukewarm interest, while a thoughtfully crafted one can spark enthusiasm and set the stage for what is to come.

The registration process is another crucial moment. It should be seamless, intuitive and aligned with the overall experience you want to create. If your event is about innovation, then the registration process should reflect that, perhaps through the use of cutting-edge technology or a personalised touch that makes each attendee feel valued. On the other hand, a cumbersome or confusing registration process can frustrate attendees before they even arrive; diminishing the excitement you have worked to build.

Pre-event communications, whether they are emails, social media posts, or even personalised messages are your chance to build momentum. These touchpoints should not only provide necessary information but also reinforce the event's narrative. Share stories, highlight key speakers and offer glimpses of what attendees can expect. Each communication should be a piece of the larger puzzle, creating a cohesive and compelling story that draws your audience in.

Sensory Engagement: Beyond the Visual

When we talk about creating memorable experiences, sensory engagement is a critical factor. Human memory is deeply connected to our senses, what we see, hear, touch, taste and smell can evoke strong emotions and create lasting memories. The most successful events are those that engage multiple senses, creating a rich tapestry of experiences that resonate on a deeper level.

Visual elements are often the most obvious, but they should be more than just aesthetically pleasing. The visual design of your event - its branding, colour scheme and overall aesthetic - should align with the event's theme and objectives. Whether it is the lighting that sets the mood, the layout of the space that guides movement, or the branding that ties everything together, each visual element should contribute to the story you are telling.

But do not stop at the visual. Consider the auditory experience as well. What do attendees hear when they enter the venue? Is it a carefully curated playlist that sets the tone, or the ambient sounds of a bustling environment that energises the space? Sound can influence mood and energy levels, creating either a calming atmosphere or an invigorating one, depending on what you want to achieve.

Touch is another powerful sense that can enhance the attendee experience. Think about the materials and textures attendees will interact with - the feel of a well-crafted programme in their hands, the comfort of the seating, the smoothness of the surfaces they touch. These tactile elements, though often overlooked, can contribute to a sense of quality and attention to detail that enhances the overall experience.

Taste and smell are equally potent. The catering at your event is more than just a meal; it is an opportunity to delight the senses and reinforce your event's theme. Whether it is a gourmet dinner that reflects the sophistication of a high-end gala or creative, locally sourced snacks that highlight sustainability at an environmental conference, food and drink should be considered as part of the overall experience. Even the aroma of freshly brewed coffee in the morning can evoke a sense of comfort and hospitality, setting a positive tone for the day.

The Role of Storytelling

At the heart of every memorable event is a compelling story. Storytelling is not just about the content of the presentations or the speeches given by keynote speakers; it is about the narrative that weaves through the entire event, creating a cohesive and engaging experience.

Every event tells a story - whether it is the story of an industry's evolution, the journey of a company, or the vision of a community coming together. As an event organiser, your role is to craft this narrative, guiding attendees through an experience that is not just informative but also emotionally resonant.

The story begins with the event's theme, which serves as the central thread that ties everything together. This theme should be reflected in every aspect of the event, from the content of the sessions to the design of the space. For example, if your event is focused on innovation, the story might centre around the idea of transformation - how new technologies are changing the industry, how companies are adapting and what the future holds. This narrative can be reinforced through keynote speeches that highlight breakthrough innovations, panel discussions that explore the challenges of change and workshops that offer hands-on experience with new tools and technologies.

But storytelling is not just about the big picture; it is also about the details. Every element of the event should contribute to the narrative. The design of the stage, the flow of the agenda, the choice of speakers, all of these elements are like chapters in a book, each one building on the last to create a complete story.

Consider also the power of personal stories. Attendees connect deeply with personal experiences, whether they are shared by speakers, showcased in videos, or told through interactive exhibits. These stories humanise the content, making it relatable and impactful. They remind attendees that behind every statistic or trend, there are real people with real experiences.

As you craft the narrative of your event, think about the journey you want your attendees to take. What emotions do you want them to feel? What insights do you want them to gain? How do you want them to reflect on the experience after the event is over? By answering these questions, you can create a story that not only engages your audience during the event but also stays with them long after they leave.

Creating Touchpoints of Connection

A memorable event is one where attendees feel connected, not just to the content, but to each other. Creating opportunities for connection is essential to fostering a sense of community and ensuring that your event has a lasting impact.

Networking is often cited as one of the most valuable aspects of attending an event, but it does not happen by accident. It requires intentional design - creating spaces, moments and opportunities for attendees to connect in meaningful ways. This could be through structured networking sessions, interactive workshops, or simply the way the venue is laid out to encourage casual conversations.

But connection goes beyond just networking. It is about creating touchpoints throughout the event that bring people together. This might be a shared experience, like a group activity or a live performance, which creates a sense of camaraderie among attendees. It could be a discussion roundtable where participants can share their perspectives and learn from each other. Or it could be a digital platform that allows attendees to continue the conversation long after the event is over.

Consider also the role of personalisation in fostering connection. When attendees feel that the event is tailored to their interests and needs, they are more likely to engage and connect. This could be as simple as offering customised agendas based on attendee preferences or as complex as creating personalised content recommendations or networking opportunities. The goal is to make each attendee feel seen, valued and connected to the event and the community it brings together.

Chapter Summary

Crafting a memorable experience is about more than just executing a well-organised event; it is about creating a journey that resonates with your attendees on multiple levels. From the first impression to the final farewell, every touchpoint is an opportunity to engage the senses, tell a compelling story and foster connections that leave a lasting impact.

By focusing on sensory engagement, storytelling and creating meaningful connections, you can ensure that your event is not just an experience but an unforgettable moment that attendees will carry with them long after the event concludes. As we continue through this book, we will delve deeper into the specific tactics and strategies that can help you create such experiences, but always with the understanding that at the heart of every great event is the desire to connect, to inspire and to leave a lasting impression.

Chapter 3: Building a Network of Influence

In the dynamic world of events, success often hinges on the strength of your network. The most impactful events are not created in isolation; they are the result of strategic partnerships, well-maintained relationships and active engagement with both corporate and community stakeholders. In this chapter, we delve into the critical aspects of building a network of influence, exploring the role of partnerships, the importance of a meticulously maintained contact database - your Black Book - and strategies for engaging both corporate entities and the local community.

The Role of Partnerships: Leveraging Alliances and Collaborations for Event Success

Partnerships are the lifeblood of successful events. They provide the resources, expertise and reach that can elevate an event from good to exceptional. But not all partnerships are created equal; the most effective ones are those that are strategically aligned with your event's goals and values.

Consider the role of partnerships as building a powerful alliance - a coming together of strengths that creates something greater than the sum of its parts. In the context of events, partnerships can take many forms: from co-hosting arrangements and media collaborations to sponsorship deals and content partnerships. Each type of partnership offers unique benefits and understanding how to leverage them effectively is key to maximising their impact.

One of the most significant benefits of partnerships is the access they provide to additional resources. Whether it is financial backing, access to a broader audience, or shared expertise, the right partner can bring invaluable assets to your event. For instance, a partnership with a well-established brand can not only enhance the credibility of your event but also expand your reach to new demographics. Similarly, collaborating with a media partner can amplify your event's visibility, ensuring that your message is heard far and wide.

However, the value of partnerships goes beyond just resources; it lies in the synergy that comes from aligning with organisations that share your vision. When selecting partners, it is crucial to ensure that there is a clear alignment of goals and values. This alignment creates a foundation of trust and mutual respect, which is essential for a successful collaboration.

Take, for example, an event focused on sustainability. Partnering with organisations that are leaders in green initiatives not only reinforces the event's theme but also brings credibility and authenticity to your message. These partners can provide content, speakers and even funding that align with the event's objectives, creating a cohesive and compelling experience for attendees.

But partnerships are not just about aligning brands - they are about building relationships. The most successful event partnerships are those that are nurtured over time, based on open communication, mutual benefit and a shared commitment to success. This requires regular engagement with your partners, ensuring that their needs are met and that there is a clear understanding of each party's role and expectations.

Listening and engaging with genuine interest is key to building these relationships. When you take the time to understand what drives your partners, what they need to achieve from the collaboration, what challenges they face, you can connect on a deeper level. This level of engagement is what transforms a partnership from a transactional arrangement into a true alliance.

Strategically, partnerships should be seen as long-term investments. A successful partnership in one event can pave the way for future collaborations, creating a network of allies who are invested in your success. By building and maintaining these alliances, you create a strong foundation for your events, ensuring that you have the support and resources needed to achieve your goals.

Creating a Black Book: Developing a Database of Key Contacts and Stakeholders

In the world of event management, your Black Book is one of your most valuable assets. It is more than just a list of contacts; it is a carefully curated database of key stakeholders, influencers and decision-makers who can help you achieve your objectives. A well-maintained Black Book is the result of years of networking, relationship-building and strategic thinking.

Imagine your Black Book as a dynamic, living document that evolves over time. It includes not just names and contact details, but also notes on each individual's interests, preferences and past interactions. This level of detail allows you to tailor your approach to each contact, ensuring that every interaction is personalised and impactful.

The first step in building your Black Book is to identify the key stakeholders for your events. These might include potential sponsors, media contacts, industry influencers and community leaders. Each of these stakeholders plays a critical role in the success of your event and understanding their needs and motivations is crucial.

As you develop your Black Book, it is important to think strategically about the relationships you are building. Who are the decision-makers in the organisations you are targeting? Who has the influence to help you achieve your goals? And perhaps most importantly, how can you add value to these relationships?

One of the most effective ways to add value is by becoming a connector. By introducing key contacts to each other, facilitating collaborations and sharing opportunities, you position yourself as a valuable resource in your network. This not only strengthens your relationships but also increases the likelihood that others will reciprocate, opening doors for you when you need them.

Maintaining your Black Book requires regular attention. It is not enough to simply collect contacts; you need to stay engaged with your network. This means regularly reaching out to your contacts, whether it is to share relevant information, check in on their latest projects, or simply keep the lines of communication open. Regular engagement ensures that your relationships remain strong and that you stay top-of-mind with your contacts.

The art of follow-up is crucial here. After making a connection at an event, personalised follow-up is essential. Rather than sending a generic message, reference your previous discussion, suggest a follow-up meeting, or offer something of value related to their interests or needs. This thoughtful approach shows that you are invested in the relationship and helps maintain momentum.

In addition to regular engagement, it is important to keep your Black Book up to date. People change roles, organisations evolve and new influencers emerge. By regularly updating your database, you ensure that your network remains relevant and that you are always connected to the right people.

Strategically, your Black Book is not just a tool for managing relationships; it is a key asset in achieving your event goals. Whether you are seeking sponsorship, securing speakers, or expanding your event's reach, the contacts in your Black Book can provide the support and resources you need. By investing in these relationships, you create a network of influence that can help you succeed in every aspect of event management.

Corporate and Community Engagement: Strategies for Involving Local Businesses and Communities

Successful events do not exist in a vacuum; they are deeply connected to the communities and businesses around them. Engaging with these stakeholders is essential for creating events that are not only impactful but also sustainable and rooted in the local context.

Corporate engagement is one of the most powerful ways to build support for your event. Local businesses can provide sponsorship, in-kind donations and promotional support, helping to offset costs and increase visibility. But beyond these tangible benefits, corporate engagement also creates a sense of community ownership in the event. When local businesses are involved, they become invested in the event's success, often going above and beyond to ensure it resonates with the community.

One of the most effective strategies for corporate engagement is to align your event with the business goals of your potential partners. For example, if a local business is focused on corporate social responsibility, consider how your event can contribute to their CSR objectives. This might involve partnering on a charitable initiative, incorporating sustainability practices, or providing opportunities for employee engagement. By aligning your event with the business goals of your partners, you create a win-win situation that benefits both parties.

Reciprocity plays a crucial role in these engagements. By offering value to your corporate partners, whether through exposure, networking opportunities, or alignment with their brand values, you create a foundation of mutual benefit. This reciprocity ensures that your partners are not just contributing to the event but are also receiving tangible benefits in return.

Community engagement is equally important. Involving the local community in your event not only enhances its relevance and impact but also builds goodwill and support. This can take many forms, from involving local artists and performers to collaborating with community organisations on programming or outreach.

Consider the power of a community-driven event. When the local community is involved, the event takes on a life of its own, becoming a reflection of the community's values, culture and aspirations. This not only increases attendance and participation but also creates a lasting legacy that extends beyond the event itself.

One of the most effective ways to engage the community is through inclusive and participatory planning processes. This might involve hosting community meetings, conducting surveys, or forming advisory committees that include local residents and leaders. By involving the community in the planning process, you ensure that the event meets their needs and reflects their input, fostering a sense of ownership and pride.

In addition to planning, community engagement also involves creating opportunities for local involvement during the event. This might include showcasing local talent, offering volunteer opportunities, or providing spaces for community organisations to share their work. By creating these opportunities, you not only enhance the event experience but also strengthen the bonds between your event and the community.

Strategically, corporate and community engagement is about creating a network of support that extends beyond your immediate team. By involving local businesses and communities, you build a foundation of trust, goodwill and mutual benefit that can sustain your event for years to come.

Chapter Summary

Building a network of influence is essential for the success of any event. Through strategic partnerships, a well-maintained Black Book and active corporate and community engagement, you can create a network that provides the resources, support and reach needed to achieve your goals.

Partnerships offer the resources and credibility that can elevate your event, while your Black Book serves as a vital tool for managing and leveraging relationships. Corporate and community engagement ensures that your event is rooted in the local context, creating a sense of ownership and support that extends beyond the event itself.

As you continue to build and nurture your network, remember that influence is not just about who you know, but about the relationships you build and the value you bring to those relationships. By approaching networking with intention, strategy and a focus on mutual benefit, you can create a network of influence that drives the success of your events and your career.

Chapter 4: Executing with Precision

Executing a successful event is about more than just making sure everything runs on time. It is about orchestrating a complex series of logistical and operational components, leveraging cutting-edge technology and preparing for the unexpected. The ability to execute with precision is what separates a good event from a truly exceptional one. In this chapter, we delve into the intricacies of logistics and operations, the transformative power of technology and the critical importance of robust crisis management.

Logistics and Operations: Best Practices for Managing the Complexities of Large-Scale Events

Managing the logistics and operations of a large-scale event is akin to conducting an orchestra, where every element must come together harmoniously to create a seamless experience. The complexity of this task requires not only detailed planning but also a deep understanding of the interdependencies between various aspects of the event.

At the heart of successful event logistics is the development of a comprehensive event master plan. This plan acts as a blueprint, detailing every component of the event from start to finish. It includes timelines, task assignments, venue layouts, equipment needs, transportation logistics and contingency plans. A well-constructed master plan is essential for ensuring that all team members are aligned and that every detail is accounted for.

Venue selection is a critical component of logistics. The venue must align with the event's objectives and accommodate its specific needs, including the number of attendees, the type of sessions and the technical requirements. For instance, a conference with multiple breakout sessions will need a venue with flexible spaces that can be configured in different ways. Moreover, the venue's location, accessibility and facilities must be carefully considered to ensure a positive attendee experience. Conducting a thorough site inspection well in advance allows you to assess the suitability of the venue and identify any potential challenges.

Transportation logistics, particularly for large-scale events, can be a significant undertaking. Coordinating the arrival and departure of attendees, managing parking and ensuring smooth traffic flow around the venue are critical to avoiding congestion and delays. For events with international attendees, arranging airport transfers and providing clear guidance on public transportation options can greatly enhance the attendee experience.

The operational flow of the event itself; how attendees move through the space, the timing of sessions and the management of breaks and meals, must be meticulously planned. Crowd management strategies, such as staggered session times or multiple entry points, can help prevent bottlenecks and ensure a smooth attendee experience. Additionally, the use of technology, such as mobile apps or digital signage, can guide attendees effectively, reducing confusion and enhancing the overall flow.

Vendor management is another crucial aspect of event logistics. Coordinating with caterers, audiovisual providers, decorators and other vendors requires clear communication and a well-defined timeline. Contract negotiations should include detailed service agreements, outlining expectations for setup, delivery and breakdown, as well as contingency plans in case of delays or issues. Regular check-ins with vendors leading up to the event can help ensure that everyone is on track.

The event team is the backbone of successful operations. From event planners to volunteers, every member of the team must understand their role and responsibilities. Pre-event briefings, detailed run sheets and a clear hierarchy of command help ensure that the team operates cohesively. On the day of the event, having a central command centre where the event team can coordinate and respond to issues in real-time is invaluable.

Contingency planning is not just an afterthought; it is a critical part of the logistics and operations process. Identifying potential risks and developing backup plans for key aspects of the event, such as technology failures, weather disruptions, or supply shortages, can prevent minor issues from escalating into major crises. Regularly revisiting and updating these contingency plans as the event date approaches ensures that you are prepared for any eventuality.

Technology and Innovation: How Digital Tools and Platforms Are Transforming Event Management

Technology has become a cornerstone of modern event management, offering tools that streamline operations, enhance attendee engagement and extend the reach of events beyond the physical venue. Leveraging the right technology can transform an event, making it more interactive, personalised and efficient.

One of the most significant technological advancements in event management is the integration of event management software. These platforms allow organisers to manage registrations, track attendee data, coordinate logistics and even send real-time updates to attendees. The automation of these processes not only reduces the workload on event staff but also increases accuracy and efficiency.

Mobile event apps have revolutionised the way attendees interact with events. These apps provide real-time access to event schedules, speaker bios, venue maps and networking tools. They can also be customised to offer personalised agendas, allowing attendees to curate their experience based on their interests. Push notifications can be used to send reminders, updates, or last-minute changes, ensuring that attendees are always informed.

Virtual and augmented reality (VR and AR) are emerging technologies that are beginning to make their mark on event management. VR can be used to create immersive experiences, such as virtual tours of the venue or interactive product demonstrations, while AR can enhance physical spaces by overlaying digital content onto the real world. These technologies are particularly valuable for hybrid events, where some attendees are participating remotely. By using VR and AR, you can create engaging experiences that bridge the gap between in-person and virtual attendees.

Live streaming and on-demand video content have expanded the reach of events, allowing organisers to engage with a global audience. By streaming keynote sessions, panel discussions, or even entire events, you can extend the life of your content and reach attendees who may not have been able to attend in person. This is particularly valuable for conferences and trade shows, where the content is often dense and may benefit from being revisited after the event. Additionally, live streaming can create opportunities for real-time interaction, such as Q&A sessions or polls, which can increase engagement and participation.

Data analytics is another powerful tool that can enhance event management. By collecting and analysing data from registration, mobile apps, social media and other sources, you can gain valuable insights into attendee behaviour and preferences. This data can be used to optimise everything from session scheduling to marketing strategies, ensuring that your event not only meets but exceeds expectations. For example, analysing which sessions had the highest attendance or which speakers generated the most engagement can inform decisions for future events.

The use of artificial intelligence (AI) is also becoming more prevalent in event management. AI can be used to automate tasks such as matchmaking attendees based on interests, providing personalised content recommendations, or even managing chatbots that assist with attendee inquiries. By integrating AI into your event management strategy, you can offer a more personalised and efficient experience for attendees.

However, with the increased reliance on technology comes the need for robust IT infrastructure and support. Ensuring that your Wi-Fi network can handle the demands of hundreds or thousands of connected devices is critical, as is having IT support on hand to troubleshoot any issues that arise. Cybersecurity is another important consideration, particularly if you are collecting sensitive data such as payment information or personal details. Implementing strong security protocols and regularly testing your systems can help protect against data breaches and other cyber threats.

Crisis Management: Preparing for and Navigating Unexpected Challenges

In the world of events, even the best-laid plans can be disrupted by unforeseen challenges. Whether it is a natural disaster, a technical failure, or a health emergency, the ability to respond effectively to a crisis is what sets experienced event managers apart. Crisis management is not just about reacting to problems as they arise; it is about anticipating potential risks, preparing for them in advance and executing a well-coordinated response.

To effectively manage crises, it is crucial to understand the Four Phases of Crisis Management: Mitigation, Preparedness, Response and Recovery. These phases provide a structured approach to handling crises, ensuring that every aspect of the event is considered and that the team is prepared to respond effectively.

1. Mitigation: Reducing Potential Risks

The first phase of crisis management is mitigation, which involves taking steps to reduce the likelihood or impact of potential crises. This begins with a thorough risk assessment during the planning stages of the event. Identify potential risks such as weather disruptions, technology failures, or security threats and take proactive measures to mitigate them. For example, if your event is outdoors, consider options like securing an indoor backup venue or renting weather-resistant structures. If your event relies heavily on technology, ensure that you have redundant systems in place, such as backup power supplies and additional equipment. Mitigation is about being proactive, addressing potential problems before they arise.

2. Preparedness: Planning and Training for Crisis Scenarios

Preparedness is the second phase, focusing on developing plans and training your team to respond to potential crises. This involves creating detailed crisis management plans that outline the roles and responsibilities of each team member, communication protocols and specific action steps for various scenarios. These plans should be reviewed and tested regularly, with crisis drills conducted to ensure that everyone knows how to respond. Preparedness also includes establishing relationships with key stakeholders, such as local authorities, vendors and emergency services, to ensure that support is readily available if needed.

3. Response: Executing the Plan in Real Time

The response phase is where the crisis management plan is put into action. When a crisis occurs, it is essential to act quickly and decisively. Clear communication is critical during this phase both within the event team and with attendees, vendors and other stakeholders. Designate a crisis management team leader who is responsible for making decisions and coordinating the response. This leader should have a clear line of communication with all relevant parties and should be empowered to make real-time decisions. During the response phase, it is important to keep attendees informed, manage the flow of information and ensure that the situation is handled as smoothly as possible.

4. Recovery: Returning to Normal and Learning from the Experience

The final phase, recovery, involves returning to normal operations and learning from the crisis to improve future event planning. After the immediate crisis has been resolved, it is important to assess the impact on the event and take steps to restore normalcy. This might involve rescheduling sessions, providing refunds or compensation, or addressing any damage that occurred. Additionally, conducting a post-crisis analysis is crucial. Gather feedback from the event team, attendees and other stakeholders to understand what worked well and what could have been handled better. Use these insights to refine your crisis management plans and improve your preparedness for future events.

Communication is at the heart of effective crisis management throughout all four phases. In the event of a crisis, it is crucial that all team members know their roles and responsibilities and that there is a clear chain of command. A crisis communication plan should be in place well before the event, detailing how information will be disseminated to attendees, staff and stakeholders. This plan should include pre-drafted messages for various scenarios, as well as designated spokespersons who are trained to communicate effectively under pressure. During a crisis, timely and accurate communication can prevent panic and help maintain order.

The ability to stay calm under pressure is a hallmark of effective crisis management. When a crisis occurs, your attendees will look to you and your team for guidance. It is important to project confidence and control, even if the situation is chaotic behind the scenes. This requires not only personal composure but also a well-trained team that can execute the crisis management plan without hesitation.

Real-time decision-making is often required during a crisis. This means being able to assess the situation quickly, weigh the options and implement a course of action. For example, if a keynote speaker is suddenly unable to attend, you may need to rearrange the schedule or have a backup speaker ready to step in. If a power outage occurs, you might need to shift to a manual registration process or move outdoor activities to daylight hours. The key is to have contingency plans that are flexible and adaptable, allowing you to pivot quickly when necessary.

After the crisis has been resolved, it is essential to conduct a thorough post-event analysis. This involves debriefing with your team to review how the crisis was handled, what went well and what could have been improved. Gathering feedback from attendees, vendors and other stakeholders can also provide valuable insights. The goal of this analysis is not only to learn from the experience but also to refine your crisis management strategies for future events.

Finally, it is important to recognise that crises can also present opportunities. How you handle a crisis can significantly impact the reputation of your event and your organisation. A well-managed crisis can enhance your credibility, demonstrating your ability to lead under pressure and deliver a successful event despite challenges. By preparing thoroughly, communicating effectively and responding decisively, you can turn a potential disaster into a demonstration of your professionalism and resilience.

Chapter Summary

Executing an event with precision requires a balance of meticulous planning, strategic use of technology and the ability to manage unexpected challenges. The logistics and operations of a large-scale event are complex, but with careful planning and coordination, they can be managed effectively to create a seamless experience for attendees.

Technology has revolutionised event management, offering new ways to personalise the attendee experience, streamline operations and extend the reach of your event. However, it also requires robust infrastructure and support to ensure that everything runs smoothly.

Crisis management is a critical aspect of event execution. By understanding the Four Phases of Crisis Management: Mitigation, Preparedness, Response and Recovery , you can handle unexpected challenges with confidence and ensure that your event is successful, no matter what obstacles arise.

In this chapter, we have explored the key elements of executing an event with precision. As we continue through this book, we will build on these principles, exploring how to further refine your event strategy and design to create truly unforgettable experiences.

CRISIS MANAGEMENT FRAMEWORK (CMF)

See appendix D

Crises Management Framework

Phase	Description	Key Actions	Tools & Resources
Mitigation	Steps taken to reduce the likelihood or impact of potential crises, including risk assessments and proactive measures.	Conduct risk assessments, identify potential risks, implement preventive measures.	Risk assessment tools, preventive measures, insurance policies.
Preparedness	Planning and training for potential crisis scenarios, including the development of crisis management plans and conducting crisis drills.	Develop detailed crisis management plans, train staff, establish communication protocols, conduct crisis drills.	Crisis management software, training programs, communication tools, stakeholder lists.

Response	Executing the crisis management plan in real-time, including clear communication and real-time decision-making during the crisis.	Activate crisis management team, communicate with stakeholders, execute contingency plans, manage real-time decisions.	Crisis command centre, communication platforms, real-time monitoring tools.
Recovery	Returning to normal operations post-crisis and conducting a post-event analysis to learn and improve future crisis management strategies.	Assess the impact, restore normal operations, conduct post-crisis analysis, refine crisis management plans.	Debriefing sessions, feedback tools, data analysis software, revised crisis management plans.

Chapter 5: Measuring Success

In the fast-paced world of event management, accurately measuring success is not only vital for understanding an event's impact but also crucial for guiding future decisions. This chapter will focus on defining and tracking key performance indicators (KPIs), conducting post-event analysis and sustaining momentum beyond the event. By applying rigorous metrics and continuous evaluation, you can ensure that your events consistently meet and exceed their goals.

KPIs and Metrics: Defining and Tracking Success Indicators for Events

Key Performance Indicators (KPIs) are essential metrics that gauge the effectiveness of an event against its predefined objectives. Defining the right KPIs requires a clear understanding of your event goals, whether they are financial, operational, or related to attendee satisfaction.

Common KPIs in Event Management:

1. **Attendance and Registration Metrics:**

    - **Total Registrations:** This is the total number of people who register for the event. It provides a baseline metric for assessing interest in the event.
    - **Show-Up Rate:** Calculated as the percentage of registered attendees who actually attend the event. For example, if 1,000 people register and 800 attend, the show-up rate is 80%. This metric helps assess the effectiveness of your pre-event communication and the perceived value of the event.
    - **Early Bird Registrations:** The number of attendees who register during an early bird period. This metric

can be crucial for understanding the effectiveness of early promotions and predicting overall attendance.

2. **Engagement Metrics:**

   - **Session Attendance:** Tracks how many attendees participate in each session. For example, if 500 people attend a session designed for 1,000, the session attendance rate is 50%. This metric helps identify which sessions were most and least popular.

   - **Social Media Engagement:** Includes likes, shares, comments and mentions on platforms such as Twitter, LinkedIn and Instagram. Tools like Hootsuite or Sprout Social can help track these metrics. An example KPI might be reaching 10,000 social media mentions during the event.

   - **App Engagement:** Tracks how many attendees use the event's mobile app and how they interact with it (e.g., number of downloads, active users, in-app networking and content consumption). A common metric might be the percentage of attendees who download and use the app, with a target of 70% engagement.

3. **Financial Metrics:**

   - **Revenue:** Total income generated from the event, including ticket sales, sponsorships, merchandise and other sources. If your event generated £100,000 in ticket sales and £50,000 in sponsorship, your total revenue is £150,000.

   - **Return on Investment (ROI):** Measures the financial return on the event compared to its costs. ROI is calculated using the formula:

$$ROI = \left(\frac{Net\ Profit}{Total\ Costs}\right) \times 100$$

- For example, if the net profit is £50,000 and the total cost is £100,000, the ROI is 50%.
- **Cost per Attendee:** This metric helps evaluate the cost-effectiveness of the event by dividing the total event cost by the number of attendees. If the total cost is £100,000 and there are 1,000 attendees, the cost per attendee is £100.

4. **Operational Efficiency Metrics:**

- **Budget Adherence:** Tracks how closely the event's expenses align with the budget. For example, if the budget was £200,000 and the actual spend was £210,000, the adherence rate is 95%, indicating a 5% overspend.
- **On-Time Delivery:** Measures how well the event adhered to its schedule, including session start times, registration opening and other time-sensitive activities. This can be tracked as a percentage of activities that started on time.
- **Vendor Performance:** Evaluates the performance of vendors based on criteria such as timeliness, quality of service and adherence to contract terms. A post-event vendor review could score vendors on a scale from 1 to 10, providing a metric to inform future vendor selection.

5. **Satisfaction and Feedback Metrics:**

   - **Net Promoter Score (NPS):** A metric that measures attendee satisfaction and loyalty by asking participants how likely they are to recommend the event to others on a scale from 0 to 10. An NPS is calculated by subtracting the percentage of detractors (those who score 0-6) from the percentage of promoters (those who score 9-10). For instance, if 70% of respondents are promoters and 10% are detractors, the NPS would be +60.

   - **Post-Event Surveys:** Gather qualitative feedback on the attendee experience, session content, speakers and overall satisfaction. Survey response rates and average scores for each question provide insight into attendee satisfaction.

   - **Sponsor Satisfaction:** Often assessed through follow-up meetings or surveys, where sponsors evaluate their experience and ROI from the event. A satisfaction score of 80% or higher could be a target KPI.

Tracking Metrics: To track these metrics, it is essential to use reliable data collection tools:

- **Event Management Software:** Platforms like Cvent, Eventbrite, or Whova can automatically track registration, session attendance and other key metrics.

- **Survey Tools:** Tools like SurveyMonkey or Google Forms allow for the collection of feedback and NPS data post-event.

- **Social Media Analytics:** Platforms like Hootsuite or Sprout Social track social media engagement and sentiment.

- **Financial Tracking:** Accounting software or spreadsheets can track budget adherence, revenue and cost-related KPIs.

Post-Event Analysis: The Importance of Debriefing and Learning from Each Event

After the event concludes, the critical task of post-event analysis begins. This process is essential for understanding the successes and challenges of the event and for gathering insights that will improve future events.

Conducting a Comprehensive Debrief: A thorough debrief starts with a meeting involving all key stakeholders - event planners, marketing teams, vendors and sponsors. During this meeting, review each KPI and metric in detail, discussing what worked and what did not.

For example:

- If the **show-up rate** was lower than expected, analyse potential reasons such as ineffective reminders, competing events, or inconvenient timing.
- If **social media engagement** exceeded expectations, identify what drove that success; was it a particular speaker, session, or hashtag strategy?

Stakeholder Feedback: Collect feedback from a variety of stakeholders:

- **Attendees:** Use post-event surveys to gather data on satisfaction levels, favourite sessions and areas for improvement.
- **Sponsors:** Hold one-on-one meetings or send detailed surveys to understand how well their

expectations were met and discuss future collaborations.

- **Vendors:** Conduct performance reviews to assess their contributions to the event's success and areas where they could improve.

Documenting Lessons Learned: Create a post-event report that summarises the event's performance across all metrics. This report should include:

- **Executive Summary:** A brief overview of the event, highlighting major successes and challenges.
- **KPI Analysis:** A detailed breakdown of how the event performed against each KPI.
- **Attendee and Sponsor Feedback:** Summarised feedback from surveys and meetings.
- **Recommendations:** Actionable insights for improving future events, based on the data and feedback collected.

Practical Example: If an event's **ROI** was lower than expected, the report might recommend cost-cutting measures, changes in pricing strategy, or exploring additional revenue streams such as merchandise sales or premium ticket tiers. If **session attendance** was uneven, consider revisiting the content strategy, session formats, or speaker selection for future events.

Sustaining Momentum: Strategies for Maintaining Engagement and Relationships After the Event

The period following an event is critical for maintaining the momentum generated and fostering long-term engagement with attendees, sponsors and other stakeholders.

Engagement Strategies:

- **Follow-Up Communications:** Send personalised thank-you emails to attendees, including links to session recordings, key takeaways and highlights from the event. For example, if a particular session had high engagement, highlight it in your communications to keep the conversation going.
- **Content Marketing:** Create and distribute content that extends the event's value. This could include blog posts, video recaps, infographics and white papers based on the event's sessions.
- **Online Communities:** Develop online platforms (such as LinkedIn groups, Slack channels, or dedicated forums) where attendees can continue networking and discussing event topics. For instance, a LinkedIn group focused on a specific industry trend discussed at the event can keep the dialogue alive.

Sustaining Sponsor Relationships:

- **Sponsor ROI Reports:** Provide detailed reports to sponsors, outlining the visibility and engagement they received. Include metrics such as booth traffic, logo impressions and social media mentions.
- **Regular Check-Ins:** Schedule regular meetings or calls with sponsors to discuss the event's success, gather their feedback and explore future opportunities for collaboration.
- **Exclusive Post-Event Offers:** Offer sponsors exclusive access to post-event content, additional branding opportunities in follow-up communications, or early-bird opportunities for sponsoring future events.

Leveraging Data for Future Engagement: Use the data collected during the event to segment your audience and tailor future communications. For example:

- **Personalised Content:** If an attendee engaged heavily with sessions on a particular topic, target them with related content, invitations to webinars, or early access to similar events.
- **Early Bird Promotions:** Use data on attendance trends to offer early bird discounts to segments of your audience that are likely to convert.

Preparing for the Next Event:

- **Save-the-Date Announcements:** As soon as the current event concludes, announce the next event to keep attendees engaged and build anticipation.
- **Continuous Engagement Campaigns:** Develop campaigns that keep your audience engaged year-round, such as newsletters, webinars, or smaller networking events that lead up to the next major event.

Chapter Summary

Measuring the success of an event requires a detailed, technical approach to defining and tracking KPIs, conducting rigorous post-event analysis and maintaining engagement long after the event concludes. By focusing on specific, measurable indicators, you can gain deep insights into your event's performance, identify areas for improvement and apply these learning to future events.

Through continuous engagement with attendees, sponsors and stakeholders, you can sustain the momentum of your event and build a strong foundation for future success. This chapter has provided you with the tools and techniques necessary to measure, analyse and improve your events, ensuring that each one contributes positively to your organisation's goals and bottom line.

As we proceed through this book, we will continue to build on these principles, exploring how to create events that are not only successful but also transformative for all involved.

See appendix E

Event Management Success Metrics Framework

Metric Category	KPI/Metric	Description	Example Tools/Resources
Attendance and Registration	Total Registrations, Show-Up Rate, Early Bird Registrations	Metrics that assess the total number of registrations, the percentage of attendees who show up and the effectiveness of early promotions.	Event Management Software (e.g., Cvent, Eventbrite), CRM Systems
Engagement	Session Attendance, Social Media Engagement, App Engagement	Metrics that measure attendee engagement through session participation, social media activity and interactions with the event app.	Social Media Analytics Tools (e.g., Hootsuite, Sprout Social), Mobile App Analytics
Financial Performance	Revenue, ROI, Cost per Attendee	Financial metrics that evaluate the economic success of the event, including total revenue, return on investment and cost-effectiveness	Accounting Software, Financial Dashboards
Operational Efficiency	Budget Adherence, On-Time	Metrics that evaluate the efficiency and	Project Management Software (e.g.,

	Delivery, Vendor Performance	effectiveness of event operations, including budget management, adherence to schedules and vendor performance.	Trello, Asana), Vendor Performance Reviews
Satisfaction and Feedback	Net Promoter Score (NPS), Post-Event Surveys, Sponsor Satisfaction	Feedback metrics that gauge the satisfaction of attendees and sponsors, including NPS scores, survey results and sponsor feedback.	Survey Tools (e.g., SurveyMonkey, Google Forms), Sponsor Follow-Up Interviews

The People Behind Events

When we think about events, it is easy to get caught up in the process, the operations, the staging, the meticulously planned agenda. But beneath the surface, events are fundamentally about people. They are the heartbeat of every event, the driving force behind every decision and the true essence of what makes an event successful. In this part of the book, we will shift our focus to the people - the ones who bring events to life and the ones who participate, each bringing their unique needs, desires and motivations to the table.

Events are not just a collection of roles or titles - they are a confluence of individuals, each with their own story, their own goals and their own reasons for being there. Understanding this human element is crucial to grasping the full value of attendance, both for those who produce events and those who participate in them.

The Convener

At the centre of every event is the convener, the individual who had the vision and the determination to bring people together. The convener's role is not just to organise but to inspire, to create a space where ideas can flourish and connections can be made. Conveners often have a personal stake in the event - they want to see their vision come to life, they want to facilitate dialogue and they want to make an impact. Understanding the convener's motivations helps us appreciate the passion and dedication that go into every detail of the event.

The Sponsors

Sponsors, too, are people with their own set of goals and expectations. They come to the table seeking visibility, brand alignment and a return on their investment. But beyond the corporate objectives, sponsors are individuals who believe in the value of the event. They want to connect with the audience, to be seen as leaders in their field and to build relationships that will last beyond the event. Recognising the human element in sponsorships allows us to craft partnerships that are not just transactional but genuinely collaborative.

The Participants

The participants are the lifeblood of any event. They come for varied reasons; some to learn, others to network, some to showcase their own work and others simply to be part of something bigger than themselves. Each participant brings their own expectations, hopes and ambitions. They are not just attendees; they are active contributors to the event's success. Understanding what drives participants helps us create experiences that resonate, that provide value and that make them feel seen and heard.

The Staff

Behind every successful event is a team of dedicated individuals who work tirelessly to ensure everything runs smoothly. These are the people who often go unnoticed - the event planners, the coordinators, the technicians, the support staff - but without them, there would be no event. They bring their expertise, their problem-solving skills and their commitment to the table, often working long hours to make sure every detail is perfect. Recognising the people behind the scenes reminds us of the importance of teamwork and the collective effort it takes to bring an event to life.

The Vendors

Vendors are more than just suppliers; they are partners in the event's success. Whether they are providing food, technology, decor, or entertainment, vendors bring their own creativity and passion to the table. They are entrepreneurs, small business owners and artisans who take pride in their work and who want to see the event succeed just as much as the convener does. Understanding the vendors as people helps us build stronger, more collaborative relationships that enhance the overall event experience.

The Volunteers

Volunteers often come to events with a desire to contribute, to be part of something meaningful. They bring energy, enthusiasm and a willingness to help wherever needed. Volunteers are individuals who see the value in the event and want to play a role in making it happen. They may be students, professionals, or community members, each with their own reasons for getting involved. Recognising their contributions reminds us of the importance of community and the power of collective action.

The Speakers and Performers

Speakers and performers are the voices and faces of the event. They come to share their knowledge, their art, their stories. But they, too, are people with their own aspirations - whether it is to inspire, to educate, to entertain, or to challenge. Understanding their motivations helps us create platforms where they can shine, where their message can resonate with the audience and where they feel valued and appreciated.

The Audience

Lastly, we must not forget the audience, the collective energy that drives the event forward. The audience is not a monolith; it is made up of individuals, each with their own perspectives, experiences and desires. They come to listen, to learn, to engage and to be part of the conversation. Understanding the audience as a collection of people, rather than just numbers, helps us create events that truly connect on a human level.

Understanding the Human Element

At the end of the day, events are about people - people coming together to share, to learn, to collaborate and to celebrate. Every individual involved in an event, from the convener to the audience, brings something unique to the table. Understanding what each person wants, what drives them and what they hope to achieve is crucial to creating events that are not only successful but also meaningful.

This human element is at the heart of the value of attendance. It is not just about the logistics, the speakers, or the content, it is about the connections that are made, the relationships that are built and the experiences that are shared. By unmasking the categories and seeing the people behind them, we can better understand what makes an event truly valuable for everyone involved.

As we move into Part II, let us keep this perspective in mind. Whether you are a producer or a participant, understanding the human element will help you navigate the world of events with greater empathy, insight and effectiveness. After all, it is the people who make events what they are and it is through understanding people that we can unlock the true value of attendance.

Chapter 6: The Value of Attendance

Attending events whether as a participant, sponsor, or speaker offers an array of opportunities that extend far beyond the immediate experience. The value of attendance is often measured in terms of the connections made, the knowledge gained and the doors opened to new business opportunities. This chapter explores the multifaceted benefits of event attendance, focusing on networking, knowledge acquisition, personal branding and the tangible opportunities that arise from being present.

Networking: Building and Expanding Your Professional Circle

Networking remains one of the most compelling reasons to attend events. The ability to connect with peers, industry leaders and potential clients or partners in a face-to-face setting is invaluable. While digital communication has become prevalent, the in-person connections made at events tend to be more memorable and impactful.

Strategic Networking: At the heart of effective networking is a strategic approach. It's not just about collecting business cards or shaking hands; it's about engaging in meaningful conversations that can lead to lasting professional relationships. Before attending an event, it's crucial to define your networking goals. Are you looking to connect with potential clients, seek out partnerships, or expand your industry knowledge? By identifying your goals, you can approach networking with purpose.

For example, a study by Harvard Business Review found that 95% of professionals consider face-to-face meetings essential for long-term business relationships. This statistic underscores the importance of in-person networking as a critical tool for building trust and credibility, which are essential for fostering enduring professional relationships.

Expanding Your Network: Attending events provides a unique opportunity to expand your professional circle beyond your immediate industry or geographic location. For instance, at a large conference, you might meet someone who works in a different sector but has valuable insights or connections that could benefit your business. These cross-industry connections can lead to unexpected opportunities and collaborations that wouldn't have been possible otherwise.

The Power of Face-to-Face Interaction: Despite the convenience of digital networking platforms, nothing replaces the impact of face-to-face interaction. According to a survey by Oxford Economics, 40% of prospective customers are more likely to convert into actual customers after a face-to-face meeting. When you meet someone in person, you can convey your personality, enthusiasm and professionalism in ways that are difficult to achieve through emails or video calls. This personal touch can make you more memorable and help establish a deeper connection.

Knowledge Acquisition: Gaining Insights and Staying Ahead

Another significant value of attending events is the opportunity to acquire new knowledge. Events such as conferences, seminars and workshops are designed to disseminate the latest industry trends, research and best practices. By attending these events, you gain insights that can help you stay ahead of the curve and make informed decisions for your business.

Access to Industry Leaders: Many events feature keynote speakers and panel discussions led by industry leaders and experts. These sessions provide a rare opportunity to hear directly from those at the forefront of your field. Whether it's a CEO discussing the future of the industry or a researcher presenting groundbreaking findings, these insights can be invaluable for your professional development.

For example, a study by Meetings Mean Business Coalition revealed that 91% of attendees believe that in-person meetings lead to more engaged and creative discussions, which can result in greater innovation. Attending these sessions allows you to absorb this knowledge and apply it to your work, positioning you as a leader within your own organisation.

Learning from Peers: In addition to learning from industry leaders, attending events allows you to learn from your peers. Breakout sessions, workshops and roundtable discussions are often designed to facilitate knowledge sharing among attendees. These interactive sessions enable you to hear about the challenges and successes of others in your field, offering practical advice and new ideas that you can implement in your own work.

A survey by the Professional Convention Management Association (PCMA) found that 76% of attendees believe that the networking and knowledge-sharing opportunities at events are the most valuable aspects of their experience. This highlights the importance of engaging with peers as a key component of knowledge acquisition.

Continuing Education: For many professionals, events offer a platform for continuing education. Many conferences and workshops offer certification programs or provide Continuing Professional Development (CPD) credits. These credentials not only enhance your expertise but also demonstrate your commitment to staying current in your field. The knowledge gained through these programs can be directly applied to your work, making you more effective and valuable in your role.

For example, data from the Chartered Institute of Personnel and Development (CIPD) indicates that professionals who engage in regular CPD activities are 30% more likely to achieve promotions or career advancements. This statistic underscores the tangible benefits of continuing education through event attendance.

Personal Branding: Showcasing Your Professional Identity

Personal branding is an often overlooked yet critical aspect of event attendance. In today's competitive professional landscape, how you present yourself at events can significantly impact your career trajectory. Your personal brand is the unique combination of skills, experience and personality that you bring to the table. It's how you differentiate yourself from others in your field and how you are perceived by peers, employers and clients.

Strategic Personal Branding: When attending events, it's essential to think strategically about your personal brand. Consider how you want to be perceived and what message you want to convey. Are you positioning yourself as an industry expert, a thought leader, or an innovator? Your brand should be consistent across all interactions whether in a keynote presentation, a networking session, or a casual conversation.

Leveraging Speaking Opportunities: One of the most effective ways to enhance your personal brand at events is by securing speaking opportunities. Delivering a presentation or participating in a panel positions you as an authority in your field. It allows you to showcase your expertise, share your insights and connect with a larger audience. According to the Content Marketing Institute,

92% of event marketers believe that speaking opportunities are a powerful tool for personal branding.

Professional Appearance and Communication: Your personal brand is also reflected in how you present yourself physically and verbally. Dressing appropriately for the event, maintaining a confident posture and engaging in clear, articulate communication all contribute to a strong personal brand. The importance of first impressions cannot be overstated research from Princeton University suggests that people form opinions about you within the first seven seconds of meeting.

Building a Digital Presence: In today's digital age, your online presence is an extension of your personal brand. Engaging with event content on social media, sharing your insights and connecting with other attendees online can enhance your visibility and reinforce your brand. Use platforms like LinkedIn to share your thoughts on event topics, post updates and engage with others in your industry. A strong online presence can amplify the impact of your in-person interactions, extending your reach beyond the event.

Access to Opportunities: Unlocking Doors to New Ventures

The value of attendance also lies in the opportunities that arise from being in the right place at the right time. Events are fertile ground for discovering new business ventures, partnerships and collaborations. By positioning yourself at the centre of industry gatherings, you increase your chances of encountering opportunities that can propel your career or business forward.

Spotting Trends and Innovations: Events are often where new trends and innovations are first introduced. Whether it's a trade show where companies unveil their latest products or a conference where thought leaders discuss emerging technologies, attending these events keeps you at the cutting edge of your industry. By staying informed about the latest developments, you can identify opportunities for your business to innovate or adapt.

According to research by Frost & Sullivan, companies that are early adopters of new technologies introduced at industry events are 30% more likely to outperform their competitors. This statistic highlights the importance of being present at events where the latest trends and innovations are showcased.

Building Strategic Partnerships: Events provide a unique environment for building strategic partnerships. The informal setting of networking events, dinners and receptions allows you to connect with potential partners in a more relaxed and personal way. These interactions can lay the groundwork for future collaborations, whether it's a joint venture, a strategic alliance, or a co-marketing initiative.

A study by the Event Marketing Institute found that 74% of business leaders believe that partnerships formed at events are more productive and long-lasting than those formed through other means. This underscores the value of using events as a platform to build strategic alliances.

Access to Decision Makers: One of the most significant advantages of attending events is the access it provides to decision-makers. Whether you're trying to pitch a new product, secure a partnership, or gain a new client, being able to speak directly to the key decision-makers in an informal setting can significantly increase your chances of success. These interactions, which might take weeks or months to arrange through formal channels, can happen spontaneously at an event.

Generating Leads and Sales: For many businesses, events are a prime opportunity to generate leads and close sales. Trade shows, in particular, are designed to connect buyers and sellers, making them an ideal environment for showcasing your products or services. Even if you don't make an immediate sale, the leads you generate at an event can be nurtured into long-term customers.

According to a report by the Centre for Exhibition Industry Research (CEIR), 77% of decision-makers found at trade shows make at least one new purchase based on what they saw. This statistic highlights the direct link between event attendance and generating sales.

Chapter Summary

The value of attendance at events is multifaceted, offering opportunities for networking, knowledge acquisition, personal branding and unlocking new ventures. By attending events, you position yourself at the heart of industry activity, where the most significant connections are made, the latest knowledge is shared and the most promising opportunities.

Chapter 7: Maximising Event ROI for Participants

Attending an event is an investment of both time and resources and like any investment, it's crucial to ensure you receive a return. Maximising the return on investment (ROI) for participants involves strategic preparation, effective engagement during the event and leveraging the connections made afterward. This chapter provides a comprehensive guide on how to achieve the highest ROI from event participation by focusing on pre-event preparation, engaging effectively and leveraging your network post-event.

Pre-Event Preparation: Researching and Setting Objectives

Success at any event begins long before you walk through the doors. The key to maximising your ROI is thorough preparation, which includes researching the event, setting clear objectives and planning your strategy.

Researching the Event: Before attending an event, it's important to conduct in-depth research. This involves understanding the event's theme, the key speakers, the schedule and, most importantly, the attendee list. Knowing who will be present allows you to identify potential contacts, partners, or clients who align with your business goals. Tools like LinkedIn can be invaluable for identifying attendees, researching their backgrounds and even initiating connections before the event.

For example, if you're attending an industry conference, research the keynote speakers and session topics to identify which ones align with your professional interests or knowledge gaps. If certain companies or individuals are of particular interest, make a note to attend sessions where they are speaking or participating in panels.

Setting Clear Objectives: Once you have a clear understanding of the event, the next step is to set specific, measurable objectives. These objectives should be aligned with your overall business or career goals. Are you attending to generate leads, learn about industry trends, build partnerships, or enhance your personal brand? Each of these goals requires a different approach, so it's crucial to be clear about what you want to achieve.

For example, if your goal is to generate leads, your objectives might include meeting a specific number of potential clients, collecting a certain number of business cards, or setting up follow-up meetings. If your goal is to learn, your objectives could involve attending specific sessions and taking notes on key takeaways that can be applied to your work.

Planning Your Strategy: With your objectives in mind, develop a strategy for the event. This includes planning which sessions to attend, which networking events to prioritise and how to manage your time effectively. Consider scheduling meetings with key contacts in advance to ensure you make the most of your time.

Additionally, prepare your personal pitch; how you will introduce yourself and explain your purpose at the event. Having a concise and compelling introduction can help you make a strong first impression and set the tone for meaningful interactions.

The Pre-Event ROI Maximisation Framework

1. **Identify Key Opportunities**: Research the event agenda, identify key sessions, speakers and attendees who align with your goals.

2. **Set SMART Goals**: Define Specific, Measurable, Achievable, Relevant and Time-bound goals for the event.
3. **Plan Strategic Engagement**: Map out which sessions to attend, who to meet and how to interact with them. Schedule meetings if possible.
4. **Prepare Your Pitch**: Develop and rehearse your elevator pitch, ensuring it is aligned with your goals and the context of the event.

This framework helps ensure that your efforts are focused and that you are fully prepared to make the most of the event.

Engaging Effectively: Tips for Meaningful Interactions and Follow-Ups

Engagement is at the heart of maximising your ROI at events. The way you interact with others during the event can make a significant difference in the outcomes you achieve. Effective engagement involves not just initiating conversations but also following up in a way that builds lasting relationships.

Making Meaningful Connections: At the event, focus on quality over quantity when it comes to networking. It's better to have a few meaningful conversations than to collect dozens of business cards without any real connection. Engage others by asking insightful questions, listening actively and finding common ground. Remember, networking is not just about what others can do for you, but also about how you can provide value to them.

For example, if you meet someone who could be a potential partner, discuss how your businesses might complement each other. If you meet someone who is facing challenges that you've encountered before, offer your insights or resources. These gestures of value can help cement the connection and lay the groundwork for a lasting professional relationship.

Maximising Session Engagement: When attending sessions, be an active participant. Ask questions during Q&A segments, engage with speakers afterward and share your insights on social media using event hashtags. This not only enhances your learning experience but also increases your visibility at the event. Engaging with the content and the speakers demonstrates your interest and can open doors to further discussions and connections.

Effective Follow-Up: The real work of networking begins after the event ends. Follow-up is critical to turning event contacts into valuable relationships. Send personalised follow-up emails to the people you connected with, referencing your conversation to reinforce the connection. If possible, suggest a follow-up meeting or call to explore potential collaborations.

For example, if you discussed a particular project or idea with someone, mention it in your follow-up and propose a next step. This could be as simple as scheduling a coffee meeting or as detailed as outlining a potential partnership plan. The key is to keep the momentum going and show that you're serious about continuing the conversation.

Utilising Technology for Follow-Up: Leverage technology tools such as CRM systems to track your contacts and follow-ups. Many CRM systems allow you to set reminders for follow-ups, categorize contacts based on their potential value and keep notes on previous interactions. This ensures that no valuable connection slips through the cracks.

The Event Engagement Framework

1. **Be Present**: Engage fully during sessions and networking opportunities, ensuring you make meaningful connections.
2. **Value Exchange**: Focus on how you can add value to each interaction, whether through knowledge, resources, or introductions.
3. **Active Participation**: Contribute to discussions, ask questions and use social media to share insights and connect with others.
4. **Structured Follow-Up**: Use CRM tools to organize and schedule follow-ups, ensuring that you maintain momentum and deepen relationships.

This framework provides a structured approach to engaging effectively during the event and ensuring that your interactions lead to valuable outcomes.

Leveraging the Black Book: How to Use the Contacts Made at Events to Your Advantage

One of the most valuable outcomes of attending events is the expansion of your professional network, often referred to as your "Black Book" of contacts. Leveraging these contacts effectively can significantly enhance your ROI.

Organising Your Contacts: After the event, organise your new contacts systematically. Categorise them based on their relevance to your objectives such as potential clients, partners, or mentors. Use a CRM tool or even a simple spreadsheet to track details like where you met, the context of your conversation and any follow-up actions.

Building Long-Term Relationships: The key to leveraging your Black Book is to focus on building long-term relationships rather than seeking immediate gains. Regularly engage with your contacts through emails, social media, or even casual check-ins. Share valuable content, such as industry insights or articles, which could be of interest to them. This keeps you on their radar and reinforces your relationship over time.

Strategic Collaboration: Identify opportunities for strategic collaboration with your contacts. This could involve co-hosting events, collaborating on projects, or even cross promoting each other's businesses. Strategic collaborations can provide mutual benefits and strengthen your professional ties.

For example, if you met a potential partner at a trade show, explore ways to collaborate on a joint venture or marketing campaign. This not only benefits both parties but also maximises the value of the connection made at the event.

Referrals and Recommendations: A strong network can also be a source of referrals and recommendations. If you've established trust and rapport with your contacts, they may refer you to others in their network or recommend you for opportunities. This can lead to new clients, partnerships, or even job offers, significantly boosting your ROI from the event.

The Post-Event Networking Framework

1. **Categorise Contacts**: Organize your contacts based on potential value and relevance to your objectives.

2. **Ongoing Engagement**: Regularly engage with your contacts, providing value through insights, introductions, or collaborative opportunities.

3. **Strategic Collaborations**: Identify and pursue opportunities for partnerships or joint ventures that benefit both parties.

4. **Referral Network**: Build and maintain a network of trusted contacts who can refer and recommend you for new opportunities.

This framework ensures that the connections you make at events continue to provide value long after the event has ended.

Chapter Summary

Maximising ROI from event participation requires a strategic approach that begins with thorough preparation, continues with effective engagement during the event and extends into post-event follow-ups and relationship-building. By setting clear objectives, engaging meaningfully and leveraging the connections made, you can ensure that your investment in attending events yields significant returns.

Whether your goal is to generate leads, build partnerships, or enhance your personal brand, the strategies and frameworks outlined in this chapter provide a roadmap for achieving those outcomes. As you continue to apply these techniques, you'll find that your ability to extract value from event participation will grow, making each event a more productive and rewarding experience.

EVENT ENGAGEMENT MODEL (EEM)

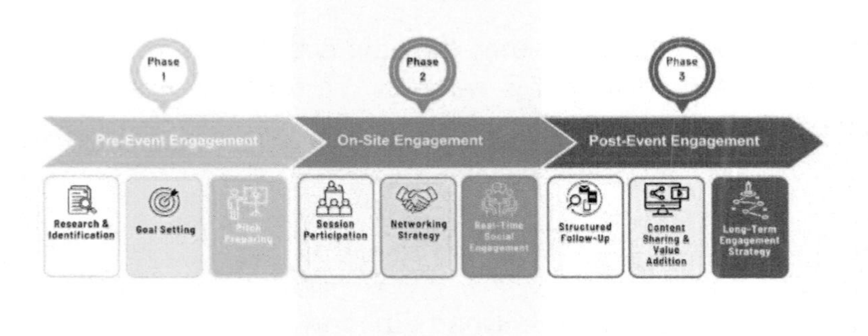

See appendix A

Event Engagement Model (EEM)

Stage	Actions
Pre-Event Engagement	Research & Identification Goal Setting Pitch Preparation
On-Site Engagement	Session Participation Networking Strategy Real-Time Social Engagement
Post-Event Engagement	Structured Follow-Up Content Sharing & Value Addition Long-Term Engagement Strategy

Chapter 8: Strategic Attendance

Attending events is not just about being present; it is about being strategically present. The difference between simply showing up and truly participating can have a significant impact on your professional growth, the relationships you build and the opportunities you unlock. In this chapter, we will explore how to choose the right events that align with your goals, understand the nuances of different event formats and harness the power of corporate sponsorship and participation to maximise your impact.

Choosing the Right Events: How to Identify Which Events Align with Your Professional Goals

The journey to choosing the right events begins with a deep understanding of your professional goals. Imagine you are at a crossroads, each path leading to a different destination. One path may take you towards career advancement, another towards expanding your network and yet another towards learning new skills or exploring business opportunities. Your destination or your goals should guide the path you choose.

If your primary objective is career advancement, you might find yourself drawn to events that offer access to industry leaders. These could be high-profile conferences, trade shows, or professional development workshops where the thought leaders of your field congregate. These events are not just about soaking in information; they are about positioning yourself among the movers and shakers, learning from them and showcasing your own expertise in the process.

On the other hand, if expanding your network is your main focus, the landscape changes. You would look for events that attract a diverse group of professionals, possibly within your industry or across related fields. Networking-focused events like roundtables, mixers, or annual meetings of industry associations are like rich fishing grounds, teeming with the potential to connect with the right people; those who could become collaborators, mentors, or clients.

For those whose goals centre around learning and development, the key is to find events that promise high-quality educational content. Workshops, seminars, or conferences that delve into the latest trends, technologies and best practices in your field are where you need to be. These are not just opportunities to learn but to also engage in deep conversations, ask questions and perhaps even challenge the status quo.

Choosing the right events is also about evaluating their quality and fit. You would not buy a ticket to just any show without knowing if it is worth your time, would you? Similarly, you need to assess the reputation of the event and its track record. Has it been successful in the past? What do previous attendees have to say about it? Positive feedback and strong testimonials are good indicators that an event will deliver value.

But it is not just about the event itself; it is also about who will be there. The audience profile is a critical factor. Are the attendees the kind of people you want to connect with? Will they help you achieve your networking or business goals? Sometimes, the value of an event lies not in the content but in the people you meet.

Then there is the content and speaker lineup. A well-curated agenda with high-quality speakers can make all the difference. These are the voices you will be learning from, the minds that will challenge and inspire you. Make sure their expertise and the topics they cover align with your interests and goals.

Finally, consider the logistics. The location, timing and costs associated with attending an event can either make it a breeze or a burden. You need to weigh the potential benefits against the logistical challenges to make an informed decision. Sometimes, it is worth traveling across the country for a few days if the event promises substantial returns; other times, a local event might offer just what you need without the hassle.

Once you have identified the events that seem to align with your goals, the next step is to prioritise them. It is easy to feel overwhelmed by the sheer number of events out there, so it is important to create an event calendar for the year. This helps you plan ahead, avoid conflicts and make sure you are dedicating your time and resources to the most valuable opportunities.

Balance is key. You want to diversify your event attendance by exploring different types of events, but you also need to stay focused. Attending too many events can dilute your efforts, while attending too few may limit your opportunities. Set specific attendance goals for each event, whether it is the number of new connections you want to make, the sessions you want to attend, or the outcomes you aim to achieve. Having clear goals keeps you focused and ensures that you maximise the value of your attendance.

Round Tables, Conferences and Galas: Understanding the Nuances and Benefits of Different Event Formats

Not all events are created equal and understanding the nuances of different event formats allows you to tailor your approach to each one. Each format offers unique opportunities and requires a different strategy to make the most of it.

Round tables, for instance, are usually smaller, more intimate gatherings that focus on discussion and collaboration among a select group of participants. Picture a group of industry experts seated around a table, sharing insights and debating ideas. This format is ideal for deepening relationships and engaging in meaningful conversations with peers and leaders. The real value here lies in the quality of the dialogue, not the quantity of people you meet.

The benefits of round tables are clear: they offer a chance for direct interaction with key players in your industry, allowing you to contribute your own insights and establish yourself as a knowledgeable professional. When attending a round table, preparation is key. Come ready with specific topics or questions you want to discuss. Engage actively in the conversation, listen to others and be open to different perspectives. These intimate settings are where you can truly shine, so make sure you are contributing thoughtfully and building strong, collaborative relationships.

Conferences, on the other hand, are a different beast altogether. These are larger-scale events that bring together professionals from across an industry or sector. Imagine walking into a massive convention centre, filled with booths, stages and buzzing with energy. Conferences typically feature a combination of keynote speakers, panel discussions, workshops and networking sessions. The scale and diversity of these events provide access to a broad range of industry insights, trends and innovations.

At a conference, the opportunities for networking are vast, but so is the potential for getting lost in the crowd. To maximise your ROI, it is crucial to plan your schedule in advance. Identify the sessions that align with your goals and make time for networking events. Engage with speakers and fellow attendees, take notes on key insights and be proactive in following up with new contacts. Conferences are as much about the connections you make as they are about the content you consume.

Then there are gala events - those formal, social gatherings that often include a dinner, awards ceremony and entertainment. Galas may not offer the same educational content as conferences or round tables, but they provide a unique opportunity for networking and brand visibility in a more relaxed and celebratory atmosphere.

Imagine walking into a beautifully decorated ballroom, the sound of clinking glasses and soft music filling the air. You are there not just to enjoy the evening, but to build relationships in a more informal setting. Galas are excellent for strengthening existing relationships and opening doors to new opportunities. The key is to focus on relationship-building rather than formal business discussions. Engage in conversation with a wide range of attendees, get to know them on a personal level and enjoy the evening. The connections you make here can pave the way for future business interactions.

Corporate Sponsorship and Participation: How Businesses Can Gain Exposure and Build Relationships by Attending or Sponsoring Events

For businesses, events offer an unparalleled opportunity to gain exposure, build relationships and reinforce brand positioning. Corporate sponsorship and participation can amplify these benefits, providing a platform for companies to connect with their target audience, showcase their expertise and build long-lasting relationships.

Corporate sponsorship is a powerful tool for businesses looking to enhance their visibility and credibility within their industry. By sponsoring an event, companies can align their brand with a particular cause, industry, or community, positioning themselves as leaders in their field. The visibility that comes with sponsorship is significant; your company's logo, messaging and representatives are prominently displayed throughout the event, leading to increased brand awareness and recognition among your target audience.

But sponsorship is not just about slapping your logo on a banner. It is about engaging with the audience in a meaningful way. Sponsorship often includes opportunities for direct engagement, whether through speaking opportunities, branded content, or interactive displays. This engagement can lead to meaningful connections and generate leads for your business. Additionally, associating your brand with a reputable event can enhance your company's credibility and trustworthiness, signalling to the audience that you are invested in the industry and are a key player in the conversation.

However, beyond sponsorship, active participation in events is essential for businesses looking to maximise their ROI. This participation can take many forms, from attending as a delegate to hosting a booth or speaking at a session. Active participation allows your company representatives to network with potential clients, partners and industry peers. These relationships can lead to new business opportunities, collaborations and partnerships.

Moreover, events provide a platform to showcase your company's expertise. Speaking opportunities, panel discussions and workshops are chances to demonstrate your thought leadership, share insights and attract interest from potential clients and partners. Attending events also keeps your company informed about industry trends, challenges and innovations, which can inform your business strategy and help you stay ahead of the competition.

To maximise the ROI of your company's sponsorship and participation, it is important to approach these opportunities strategically. Before sponsoring or participating in an event, define clear objectives for what you want to achieve. This could include lead generation, brand visibility, or market research. Having clear goals ensures that your efforts are focused and aligned with your business strategy.

Make full use of the benefits offered by sponsorship packages, such as speaking opportunities, branding placements and access to attendee lists. Tailor your messaging and engagement strategies to maximise your visibility and impact. After the event, measure the success of your sponsorship and participation against your objectives. Evaluate the leads generated, the quality of the connections made and the overall impact on your brand. Use this data to refine your approach for future events.

Chapter Summary

Strategic attendance is about more than just showing up; it is about making informed decisions that align with your goals, choosing the right events and engaging in ways that maximise your impact. Whether you are attending as an individual or representing a company, the strategies outlined in this chapter will help you approach events with purpose and intention.

We have explored how to choose the right events, understand the nuances of different event formats and harness the power of corporate sponsorship and participation. By following these strategies, you can ensure that your attendance at events is not just beneficial but truly transformative for your career or business.

As you continue to navigate the world of events, remember that every decision from the events you attend to how you engage can significantly impact your professional journey.

By being strategic, intentional and informed, you can turn every event into an opportunity for growth, success and lasting impact.

Chapter 9: The Global Perspective

The ability to navigate global events is no longer just a competitive advantage, it's a necessity. Whether you are attending or organising events across borders, understanding the nuances of international interactions is crucial to achieving success. In this chapter, we will explore best practices for navigating international events, the importance of cultural intelligence in networking and the vital role that global events play in economic diplomacy. Additionally, I will introduce the Global Connection Framework, a comprehensive product designed to help organisations establish and optimise global partnerships.

Navigating International Events: Best Practices for Attending and Organising Across Borders

Attending or organising an event in a foreign country presents a unique set of challenges and opportunities. The logistical considerations, legal requirements and cultural differences can be daunting, but with the right strategies, these challenges can be turned into opportunities for growth and connection.

Strategic Planning and Preparation: When attending an international event, preparation is key. Start by understanding the local context, research the host country's business environment, political climate and cultural norms. This will help you tailor your approach to the event and ensure that you can navigate any potential challenges with confidence.

If you're organising an event, the planning process must take into account not only the logistics of bringing together participants from different countries but also the legal and regulatory frameworks of the host nation. For example, understanding visa requirements, local tax laws and contractual obligations can prevent costly misunderstandings and delays.

Leveraging Local Expertise: One of the best strategies for successfully navigating international events is to partner with local experts. Whether it's hiring a local event planner or working with a local business association, these partners can provide invaluable insights into the local market, cultural practices and logistical considerations. They can also help you build connections with local stakeholders, which can be crucial for the success of your event.

For example, when I was organising a large-scale conference in Dubai, partnering with a local agent helped us navigate the complex regulatory environment and secure the necessary permits far more efficiently than we could have on our own. This partnership not only saved time and resources but also ensured that our event was culturally sensitive and well-received by local participants.

Adapting to Local Norms: Understanding and adapting to local customs and norms is critical when attending or organising international events. This includes everything from the appropriate dress code to the etiquette of business meetings and negotiations. For instance, in Japan, business cards are exchanged with great formality and the way you present and receive a card can significantly impact the perception of your professionalism.

Incorporating local customs into the event's design can also enhance the experience for attendees. This could be as simple as including local cuisine in the catering or as complex as aligning the event's schedule with local cultural or religious observances. These small touches demonstrate respect for the host culture and can greatly enhance the success of your event.

Cultural Intelligence in Networking: Understanding and Respecting Cultural Differences

In a global context, cultural intelligence; the ability to understand and navigate different cultural norms is a critical skill for effective networking. Building strong connections across cultures requires more than just language proficiency; it requires a deep understanding of the values, communication styles and social norms of the people you are engaging with.

The Importance of Cultural Awareness: Cultural awareness involves recognising that people from different cultures may have different ways of thinking, behaving and communicating. For example, in some cultures, direct communication is valued, while in others, indirect communication is preferred. Understanding these differences can help you avoid misunderstandings and build stronger, more respectful relationships.

In a study conducted by the Harvard Business Review, it was found that 70% of international ventures fail due to cultural misunderstandings. This statistic underscores the importance of cultural intelligence in ensuring the success of international engagements.

Strategies for Developing Cultural Intelligence:

1. **Research and Education:** Before attending an international event, invest time in learning about the culture of the country. This could involve reading books, attending cultural sensitivity training, or even speaking with locals to gain insights.

2. **Active Listening:** When interacting with people from different cultures, practice active listening. Pay attention not just to what is being said but also to how it is being said. Non-verbal cues such as body

language, tone of voice and eye contact can vary significantly across cultures.

3. **Adaptability:** Be prepared to adapt your communication style and behaviour to align with the cultural norms of the people you are engaging with. This might mean being more formal in some settings or taking a more indirect approach to communication.

Building Trust Across Cultures: Trust is a foundational element of successful networking and it can be more challenging to establish across cultures. In some cultures, trust is built slowly over time through personal relationships, while in others, it can be established more quickly through professional competence. Understanding these differences and being patient in building relationships can make a significant difference in your ability to connect with others globally.

In my experience, one of the most effective ways to build trust across cultures is to demonstrate respect for the other person's culture. This could be as simple as making an effort to learn a few phrases in their language or as significant as showing a deep understanding of their cultural values and how they impact business practices.

The Role of Global Events in Economic Diplomacy: How Events Foster International Cooperation and Economic Growth

Global events play a crucial role in fostering international cooperation and driving economic growth. They provide a platform for governments, businesses and civil society to come together, share knowledge and collaborate on solutions to global challenges. In this context, events are not just about networking or knowledge exchange, they are instruments of economic diplomacy.

Global Events as Catalysts for Economic Diplomacy: Economic diplomacy involves the use of economic resources, policies and relationships to achieve foreign policy objectives. Events that bring together international stakeholders can serve as powerful tools for economic diplomacy by facilitating dialogue, building relationships and promoting trade and investment.

For example, international trade fairs and expos are often used by countries to showcase their industries, attract foreign investment and negotiate trade agreements. The World Economic Forum, held annually in Davos, Switzerland, is another example of an event that plays a significant role in global economic diplomacy. It provides a neutral platform for world leaders to discuss pressing global issues and forge partnerships that drive economic growth.

The Economic Impact of Global Events: Global events also have a direct economic impact on the host country. They create jobs, stimulate local businesses and generate revenue through tourism, hospitality and other related industries. According to the International Congress and Convention Association (ICCA), the global meetings industry generates over $1 trillion in direct spending annually, supporting millions of jobs worldwide.

In addition to the immediate economic benefits, global events can also have long-term impacts by enhancing the host country's global reputation and positioning it as a key player in international markets. This can lead to increased foreign investment, stronger trade relationships and greater influence in global economic affairs.

Introducing the Global Connection Framework: A Comprehensive Product for Facilitating Sustainable Partnerships

To effectively navigate and leverage the opportunities presented by global events, I have developed the **Global Connection Framework**. This framework is a comprehensive suite of tools, resources and services designed to help organisations establish, manage and optimise global partnerships. It is tailored to foster effective collaboration and drive sustainable development, fully aligned with the United Nations Sustainable Development Goal 17 (SDG 17): Partnerships for the Goals.

Framework Components:

1. **Strategic Partnership Development Guide:** A detailed guide to building and nurturing strategic partnerships that are aligned with your organisational goals.

2. **Collaborative Technology Platform:** A cutting-edge platform that enables seamless communication and collaboration across borders, making it easier to manage global partnerships.

3. **Capacity Building and Training Programs:** Specialised programs aimed at enhancing the skills and capabilities needed to sustain and grow global partnerships.

4. **Monitoring and Evaluation Tools:** Comprehensive tools for tracking the performance and impact of your partnerships, ensuring they deliver value over time.

5. **Consulting and Advisory Services:** Expert consulting services to help you navigate the

complexities of global partnerships, from initial setup to long-term optimisation.

This framework is not a one-size-fits-all solution but rather a flexible guide that can be tailored to different contexts and objectives. By following the Global Connection Framework, you can maximise the impact of your participation in global events and position yourself as a key player on the international stage.

Chapter Summary

Navigating international events requires a blend of strategic planning, cultural intelligence and a deep understanding of the role these events play in economic diplomacy. Whether you are attending or organising, the ability to engage effectively across cultures and leverage global connections is essential for success. By applying the Global Connection Framework, you can ensure that your participation in global events leads to meaningful connections, long-term partnerships and tangible economic benefits.

As we continue to explore the world of event management, remember that the true power of events lies not just in the connections you make but in how you use those connections to drive global collaboration and growth.

GLOBAL CONNECTION FRAMEWORK

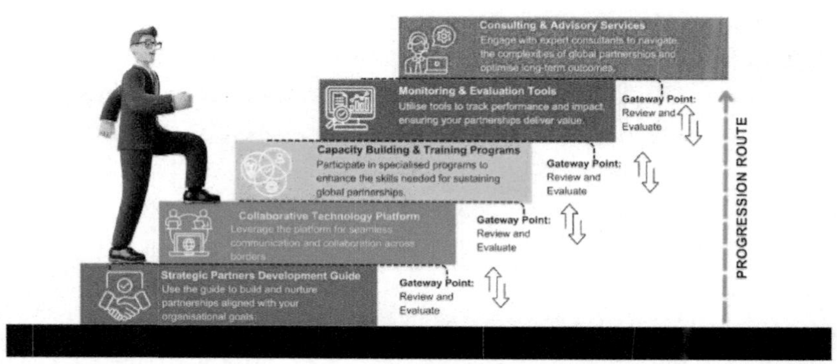

See appendix B

Global Connection Framework Outline

Component	How It Can Be Actioned
Strategic Partnership Development Guide	Use the guide to build and nurture partnerships aligned with your organisational goals.
Collaborative Technology Platform	Leverage the platform for seamless communication and collaboration across borders.
Capacity Building and Training Programs	Participate in specialised programs to enhance the skills needed for sustaining global partnerships.
Monitoring and Evaluation Tools	Utilise tools to track performance and impact, ensuring your partnerships

	deliver value.
Consulting and Advisory Services	Engage with expert consultants to navigate the complexities of global partnerships and optimise long-term outcomes.

Part III: The Expertise of Event Management

Event management is both an art and a science, requiring a blend of creativity, precision and strategic insight. As we transition into Part III of this book, we delve into the intricate expertise that defines successful event management, a field that goes far beyond the surface of logistics and operations. Here, we explore the deeper, more technical aspects of the profession, where **excellence is not just a goal but a fundamental skill** and **competence serves as the life force** that drives every successful event.

In the world of events, success is rarely accidental. It is the result of meticulous planning, informed by data and driven by a clear vision. It is about understanding not only what needs to be done, but also why it needs to be done and how it aligns with broader organisational goals. This part of the book is dedicated to unpacking the core competencies that every event professional must master, competencies that are essential to transforming an event from a mere gathering into a powerful tool for connection, influence and growth.

Technical Mastery in Event Management

At the heart of every successful event lies technical mastery, a reflection of true competence. This includes a deep understanding of event technology, from registration platforms to event apps and the ability to harness these tools to enhance the attendee experience. It also encompasses the **skilful management of budgets, timelines and resources**, ensuring that every element of the event is aligned with its objectives. In this section, we will explore the technologies and methodologies that are driving the future of event management and how they can be leveraged to create seamless, impactful experiences where **excellence is the standard**.

Strategic Thinking and Innovation

Strategic thinking is what differentiates a good event manager from a great one. It is the ability to see the bigger picture, to understand how an event fits into the larger narrative of an organisation's goals and to use that understanding to guide every decision. In this part, we will discuss how to approach event planning from a strategic perspective, using data-driven insights to inform decisions and innovate in ways that set your events apart from the competition. **Competence in strategic thinking** is not just about making informed decisions; it's about ensuring that every decision pushes the boundaries of excellence, propelling your events to new heights.

The Professionalism of Event Management

Professionalism in event management is non-negotiable. It is reflected in the way we communicate, the standards we uphold and the relationships we build. **Professional competence** is about being reliable, accountable and ethical in every aspect of our work, with **excellence** serving as the barometer by which all actions are measured. This section will cover the principles of professionalism that should guide every event manager, from dealing with clients and stakeholders to leading a team under pressure. We will also examine the critical role of crisis management in maintaining professionalism and how to prepare for and respond to unexpected challenges with grace and efficiency.

Expertise in Action

Finally, **expertise in event management is demonstrated through action**. It is about taking all the knowledge, skills and strategies we've discussed and applying them in real-world scenarios. Throughout this part of the book, you will find case studies and practical examples that illustrate how these principles are applied in practice. These examples will provide you with actionable insights that you can incorporate into your own events, helping you to elevate your work and achieve greater success. Here, **competence** becomes the engine that powers success and **excellence** becomes the result of disciplined, intentional effort.

As we move forward into the chapters that follow, I invite you to consider how each element of expertise contributes to the overall success of an event. Whether you are a seasoned professional or new to the field, the insights and strategies shared here will provide you with the tools and knowledge needed to excel in the business of events. This is where the true expertise of event management comes to life, where **strategic thinking meets technical mastery, competence drives action and professionalism ensures that every event is executed with excellence**.

Welcome to the heart of event management expertise.

Chapter 10: Core Principles of Event Management

Event management is a dynamic and multifaceted profession that requires a blend of leadership, strategic thinking and a deep understanding of diverse stakeholder needs. As we delve into the core principles of event management, we will explore the qualities that define successful event managers, the art of balancing stakeholder expectations and the importance of incorporating sustainability and corporate social responsibility (CSR) into event planning. These principles are the bedrock of effective event management and are essential for creating experiences that are impactful, inclusive and aligned with broader organisational goals.

Leadership and Vision: The Qualities that Define Successful Event Managers

At the heart of every successful event is a leader with a clear vision. Leadership in event management is not just about overseeing logistics; it's about inspiring a team, guiding stakeholders and ensuring that every aspect of the event aligns with the overarching goals. Successful event managers possess a unique blend of qualities that enable them to navigate the complexities of event planning while maintaining a focus on excellence.

Visionary Thinking: A successful event manager is a visionary, someone who can see beyond the immediate tasks and understand how the event fits into the broader organisational strategy. This involves setting clear objectives, defining the purpose of the event and ensuring that every decision made during the planning process aligns with this vision. Visionary thinking allows event managers to innovate, anticipate challenges and create events that not only meet but exceed expectations.

For example, when planning a large-scale conference, a visionary event manager will consider not just the logistics of the venue and schedule but also how the event's theme, content and design will impact attendees and achieve the desired outcomes. This holistic approach ensures that the event is not just a series of activities but a cohesive experience that resonates with participants and drives the organisation's goals forward.

Decisive Leadership: In the fast-paced world of event management, decisions often need to be made quickly and with confidence. Decisive leadership is about having the ability to assess situations rapidly, weigh the pros and cons and make informed choices that keep the event on track. This quality is especially important in high-pressure situations where time is limited and the stakes are high.

For instance, if an unforeseen issue arises, such as a key speaker cancelling at the last minute, an effective event manager must quickly determine the best course of action, whether it's finding a replacement, adjusting the schedule, or communicating the change to attendees in a way that maintains the event's integrity.

Inspirational Leadership: An event manager must also be able to inspire and motivate their team. Events are often complex projects that require the coordination of multiple teams, each with its own set of responsibilities. An inspirational leader fosters a positive working environment, encourages collaboration and ensures that everyone involved in the event is aligned with the shared vision.

This might involve regular team meetings to keep everyone informed and motivated, recognising individual and team achievements and providing support and resources to overcome challenges. An event manager who leads with inspiration and empathy can build a cohesive team that works together effectively to deliver an outstanding event.

Stakeholder Management: Balancing the Needs and Expectations of Diverse Groups

Event management involves juggling the needs and expectations of various stakeholders, from clients and sponsors to attendees and vendors. The ability to manage these relationships effectively is a core principle of successful event management. It requires a deep understanding of stakeholder priorities, excellent communication skills and the ability to find common ground between often competing interests.

Understanding Stakeholder Priorities: Each stakeholder group has its own set of priorities and expectations. For example, clients might prioritise ROI and brand visibility, while attendees may be more focused on the quality of content and networking opportunities. Sponsors are likely to be interested in brand exposure and audience engagement, while vendors need clarity on logistics and timelines.

A successful event manager takes the time to understand these varying priorities and ensures that they are addressed throughout the planning process. This might involve conducting stakeholder interviews, creating detailed briefs that outline each group's objectives and ensuring that these are reflected in the event's design and execution.

Effective Communication: Clear and consistent communication is essential for managing stakeholder relationships. This involves keeping all parties informed about the event's progress, addressing concerns promptly and ensuring that everyone has the information they need to fulfil their role effectively. Good communication helps to build trust and transparency, which are critical for maintaining positive relationships with stakeholders.

For example, regular updates via email or project management tools can keep clients and sponsors informed about milestones and any changes to the event plan. Detailed briefs and timelines can ensure that vendors understand their responsibilities and deadlines, reducing the risk of misunderstandings or delays.

Excellent Customer Service: Excellent customer service is a cornerstone of effective stakeholder management. Providing a high level of service ensures that all stakeholders feel valued and respected, which in turn fosters loyalty and long-term relationships. This involves being responsive to inquiries, addressing issues with professionalism and empathy and going the extra mile to exceed expectations.

For instance, when dealing with attendees, ensuring that their needs are met from registration to post-event follow-up can significantly enhance their overall experience. Similarly, providing personalised attention to sponsors and clients, such as customised branding opportunities or tailored sponsorship packages, can strengthen their commitment to the event and increase their satisfaction.

Negotiation and Conflict Resolution: Balancing the needs of diverse stakeholders often requires negotiation and conflict resolution. It's not uncommon for stakeholders to have competing interests and an effective event manager must be able to navigate these situations diplomatically. This involves finding compromises that satisfy all parties or, when necessary, making tough decisions that prioritise the overall success of the event.

For instance, if a sponsor requests additional branding opportunities that might conflict with the event's aesthetic or attendee experience, the event manager needs to negotiate a solution that honours the sponsor's investment while maintaining the integrity of the event. This might involve offering alternative branding options or finding creative ways to integrate the sponsor's presence without detracting from the overall experience.

Measuring Stakeholder Satisfaction: Another strategic point to consider in stakeholder management is the importance of measuring stakeholder satisfaction. Regular feedback from stakeholders helps in understanding their experience and identifying areas for improvement. Post-event surveys, one-on-one interviews and feedback forms are effective tools for gathering this information. By analysing this data, event managers can make informed adjustments and enhance future events.

Sustainability and CSR: Incorporating Corporate Social Responsibility into Event Planning

In today's world, sustainability and corporate social responsibility (CSR) are no longer optional considerations; they are essential components of successful event management. Incorporating sustainability and CSR into event planning not only enhances the event's reputation but also aligns with the growing expectations of attendees, sponsors and the wider community.

Sustainable Event Practices: Sustainable event management involves minimising the environmental impact of an event through thoughtful planning and execution. This includes everything from reducing waste and energy consumption to choosing environmentally friendly materials and venues. Sustainable practices not only benefit the environment but can also reduce costs and enhance the event's appeal to environmentally conscious attendees and sponsors.

For example, using digital invitations and event apps can reduce paper waste, while selecting venues that prioritise energy efficiency can lower the event's carbon footprint. Providing sustainable catering options, such as locally sourced or plant-based foods, can also align the event with broader sustainability goals.

Corporate Social Responsibility in Events: Incorporating CSR into event planning involves designing events that contribute positively to society. This might include partnering with local charities, supporting community initiatives, or ensuring that the event has a lasting positive impact on the local economy. CSR initiatives can enhance the event's brand and create meaningful connections with attendees and the wider community.

For instance, a conference could partner with a local charity, donating a portion of the ticket sales to support a cause aligned with the event's theme. Alternatively, the event could include volunteer opportunities for attendees, allowing them to give back to the community while participating in the event.

Measuring Impact: To ensure that sustainability and CSR initiatives are effective, it's important to measure their impact. This might involve tracking metrics such as the event's carbon footprint, waste reduction, or the amount of money raised for charity. These metrics can then be reported to stakeholders, demonstrating the event's commitment to sustainability and social responsibility.

For example, after an event, the organisers could produce a sustainability report that outlines the actions taken to reduce environmental impact, the results of these efforts and plans for future improvements. This transparency not only builds trust with stakeholders but also sets a benchmark for future events.

Chapter Summary

The core principles of event management; leadership and vision, stakeholder management, sustainability and CSR, are the foundation upon which successful events are built. These principles require a blend of strategic thinking, effective communication and a commitment to excellence. By mastering these core principles, event managers can create experiences that are not only successful but also meaningful, impactful and aligned with broader organisational and societal goals.

As we continue to explore the intricacies of event management, remember that these principles are not just theoretical concepts but practical tools that can be applied to every aspect of event planning and execution. Whether you are leading a team, balancing stakeholder expectations, or incorporating sustainability into your events, these core principles will guide you toward success.

Stakeholder Satisfaction Measurement Framework (SSMF)

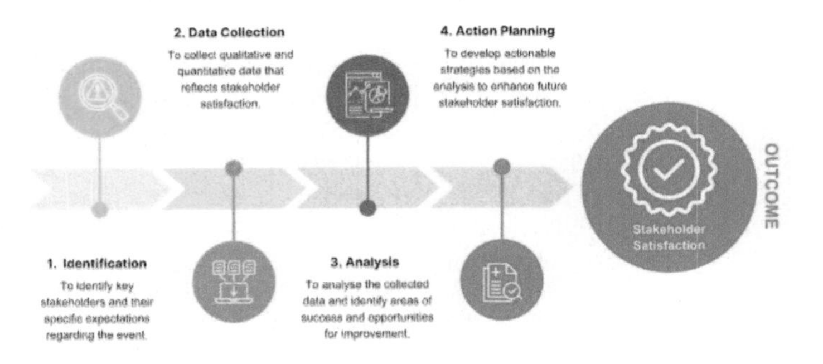

See appendix C

Stakeholder Satisfaction Measurement Framework (SSMF)

Stage	Components	Objective	Outcome
Identification	Stakeholder Mapping, Expectation Setting	To identify key stakeholders and their specific expectations regarding the event.	A clear understanding of stakeholders and their expectations.
Data Collection	Surveys and Feedback Forms, Interviews and Focus Groups, Observation and Behavioural Data	To collect qualitative and quantitative data that reflects stakeholder satisfaction.	A comprehensive set of data capturing stakeholder satisfaction.
Analysis	Quantitative Analysis, Qualitative Analysis, Benchmarking	To analyse the collected data and identify areas of success and opportunities for improvement.	A detailed understanding of strengths and areas needing attention.
Action Planning	Stakeholder Engagement Plan, Continuous Improvement Loop, Reporting and Communication	To develop actionable strategies based on the analysis to enhance future stakeholder satisfaction.	A proactive approach to enhancing stakeholder satisfaction for future events.

Chapter 11: The Dynamics of Events

Event management is a living, breathing discipline, constantly evolving to meet the needs and expectations of diverse audiences. At the heart of any successful event lies a deep understanding of its dynamics, the interplay between audience engagement, the power of content and the trends that shape the industry. In this chapter, we will explore these key elements, focusing on techniques for keeping participants invested, the importance of delivering compelling content and how staying ahead of industry trends can position your events for long-term success.

Audience Engagement: Techniques for Keeping Participants Invested and Involved

Audience engagement is more than just a buzzword; it's a critical factor that determines the success of any event. Engaged participants are more likely to have a positive experience, retain information and build lasting connections. As an event manager, your goal is to create an environment where attendees are not just passive spectators but active participants.

Understanding Your Audience: The first step in effective audience engagement is understanding who your audience is and what they want. This involves conducting pre-event surveys, analysing attendee demographics and considering the goals and interests of your participants. Whether your audience consists of industry professionals, potential clients, or the general public, tailoring your engagement strategies to their specific needs is essential.

For instance, if you're organising a technology conference, your audience might be more interested in hands-on workshops and demonstrations rather than traditional lectures. Understanding these preferences allows you to design an event that not only meets but exceeds expectations.

Interactive Sessions: One of the most effective ways to engage an audience is through interactive sessions. These can take many forms, such as Q&A sessions, live polls, workshops, or panel discussions. The key is to encourage participation by making attendees feel that their input is valuable and that they are an integral part of the event.

For example, integrating live polling tools during presentations can transform a one-way lecture into a dynamic dialogue. This not only keeps the audience engaged but also provides real-time feedback that can be used to adjust the content on the fly.

Networking Opportunities: Networking is a primary reason many people attend events, making it a crucial aspect of audience engagement. Providing structured opportunities for networking, such as speed networking sessions, roundtable discussions, or dedicated networking breaks, can enhance the overall attendee experience. These opportunities should be designed to facilitate meaningful connections rather than just casual conversations.

In addition to in-person networking, consider leveraging digital platforms to extend networking beyond the event itself. Event apps or online communities can help participants connect before, during and after the event, fostering long-term professional relationships.

Gamification: Gamification is an increasingly popular technique for boosting audience engagement. By incorporating game-like elements into your event, such as leaderboards, rewards, or challenges, you can motivate participants to engage more deeply with the content and with each other.

For example, you might create a scavenger hunt where participants earn points by attending sessions, visiting exhibitor booths, or engaging in networking activities. These points could then be redeemed for prizes or recognition, adding an element of fun and competition to the event.

Content is King: Crafting Compelling Narratives and Delivering Valuable Content

In the world of events, content truly is king. The quality of the content you deliver will significantly impact the success of your event and the satisfaction of your attendees. Crafting compelling narratives and delivering valuable content are key to creating memorable experiences that resonate with your audience.

Content Strategy: A successful content strategy begins with understanding the needs and interests of your audience. What are their pain points? What knowledge or insights are they seeking? By answering these questions, you can develop content that is relevant, informative and engaging.

When planning your event's content, think beyond traditional presentations. Consider a mix of formats such as keynote speeches, panel discussions, case studies and interactive workshops that cater to different learning styles and preferences. This diversity not only keeps the audience engaged but also allows you to cover topics from multiple angles, providing a richer experience.

Storytelling: At the core of compelling content is storytelling. Stories have the power to captivate an audience, evoke emotions and make complex information more relatable. Whether you're delivering a keynote speech or moderating a panel discussion, incorporating storytelling elements can make your content more impactful.

For example, instead of presenting dry statistics, consider framing your data within a story that illustrates real-world applications or outcomes. This approach not only makes the information more engaging but also helps the audience connect with the content on a deeper level.

Expert Speakers: The quality of your speakers can make or break your event. Choosing the right speakers, those who are not only knowledgeable but also engaging and charismatic is crucial. Expert speakers who can deliver content in a way that is both informative and inspiring will leave a lasting impression on your audience.

When selecting speakers, consider not only their expertise but also their ability to connect with the audience. A great speaker should be able to engage with participants, answer questions and adapt their presentation to the needs of the audience. Additionally, diversifying your speaker lineup can bring a range of perspectives and insights, further enriching the content of your event.

Content Delivery: How you deliver your content is just as important as the content itself. Consider the venue, the audiovisual setup and the overall environment in which your content will be presented. Ensure that your technology is reliable and that your presenters are well-prepared.

Incorporating multimedia elements such as videos, animations and interactive graphics can enhance the delivery of your content, making it more engaging and easier to understand. Additionally, providing attendees with access to content after the event, such as through recorded sessions or downloadable materials, can extend the value of your event and reinforce key messages.

Trends and Innovations: Keeping Ahead of the Curve in a Rapidly Evolving Industry

The event management industry is constantly evolving, driven by technological advancements, changing audience expectations and new trends. Staying ahead of these trends is essential for maintaining the relevance and appeal of your events. In this section, we will explore some of the key trends and innovations shaping the future of event management.

Hybrid Events: One of the most significant trends in recent years has been the rise of hybrid events, those that combine in-person and virtual elements. Hybrid events offer the flexibility to reach a broader audience, providing options for attendees who may not be able to attend in person.

To successfully execute a hybrid event, it's important to consider the needs of both in-person and virtual attendees. This might involve creating parallel content tracks, offering virtual networking opportunities and ensuring that the technology used for the virtual component is seamless and reliable. The hybrid model not only increases accessibility but also allows for greater flexibility in content delivery and audience engagement.

Sustainability in Events: Sustainability is no longer just a buzzword; it's a key consideration for many event organisers and attendees. Incorporating sustainable practices into your events, such as reducing waste, using eco-friendly materials and selecting venues that prioritise sustainability, can enhance your event's appeal and align with the values of your audience.

For example, offering digital materials instead of printed handouts, sourcing local and sustainable catering options and minimising travel by leveraging virtual attendance options are all ways to reduce the environmental impact of your event. Sustainability is not just about reducing carbon footprints; it's about creating events that are socially responsible and aligned with global efforts to combat climate change.

Personalisation: Today's attendees expect personalised experiences that cater to their individual interests and needs. This trend towards personalisation can be achieved through the use of technology, such as event apps that allow attendees to customise their schedules, receive personalised content recommendations and engage with speakers and other participants.

Personalisation extends to every aspect of the event, from the content offered to the networking opportunities provided. By using data analytics and attendee feedback, you can tailor your event to create a more relevant and engaging experience for each participant.

Technology and Innovation: Technology continues to be a driving force in the evolution of event management. Innovations such as artificial intelligence (AI), virtual and augmented reality (VR/AR) and advanced event apps are transforming how events are planned, executed and experienced.

AI can be used to personalise attendee experiences, automate event management tasks and provide real-time analytics. VR and AR offer immersive experiences that can transport attendees to virtual environments or enhance in-person events with interactive elements. Meanwhile, event apps are becoming more sophisticated, offering features such as networking tools, live polling and real-time updates.

Staying abreast of these technological advancements and incorporating them into your events can help you stay competitive and deliver cutting-edge experiences that meet the evolving expectations of your audience.

Chapter Summary

The dynamics of events are shaped by the intricate interplay of audience engagement, the quality of content and the adoption of emerging trends and innovations. By mastering these elements, event managers can create experiences that not only captivate and inspire but also drive meaningful outcomes for all stakeholders involved.

Whether you're focused on enhancing audience engagement through interactive techniques, crafting compelling content that resonates with your audience, or staying ahead of industry trends, understanding the dynamics of events is crucial to your success. As you apply the insights from this chapter, remember that the most successful events are those that balance these dynamics, creating a harmonious and impactful experience for everyone involved.

Chapter 12: The Future of Events

The events industry has always been a dynamic and ever-evolving space, but in recent years, the pace of change has accelerated dramatically. As we look to the future, it's clear that the landscape of events is being reshaped by significant global shifts, particularly in the wake of the COVID-19 pandemic. In this chapter, we will explore the key trends and developments that are set to define the future of events, focusing on the lasting impact of the pandemic, the rise of hybrid and virtual events and the economic contribution of events both in the UK and globally.

Post-Pandemic Shifts: How the Events Industry Has Changed and What's Next

The COVID-19 pandemic was a watershed moment for the events industry. The sudden halt to in-person gatherings forced a rapid pivot to virtual formats, fundamentally altering how events are conceived, planned and executed. As we emerge from the pandemic, it's clear that some of these changes are here to stay, while others will continue to evolve.

Permanent Changes in Event Formats: One of the most significant shifts resulting from the pandemic is the widespread adoption of virtual and hybrid event formats. What initially began as a necessity has now become a viable and often preferred option for many organisations. Virtual events offer unparalleled accessibility, allowing participants from around the world to engage without the constraints of travel. Hybrid events, which combine in-person and virtual elements, have become a popular choice, offering the best of both worlds.

As we move forward, it's likely that the event landscape will continue to be dominated by these flexible formats.

However, this doesn't mean the end of in-person events. Instead, we're seeing a more strategic approach to when and how these formats are used. For example, large-scale conferences might adopt a hybrid model to maximise reach, while smaller, more intimate gatherings could return to fully in-person formats to foster deeper connections.

Health and Safety as a Priority: The pandemic has also ingrained a heightened awareness of health and safety in the events industry. Even as restrictions ease, many organisers continue to implement rigorous health protocols, such as enhanced sanitation measures, contactless check-ins and air quality monitoring. These practices are likely to remain a standard part of event planning, as attendees and organisers alike prioritise safety and well-being.

In addition, the experience of the pandemic has underscored the importance of risk management and contingency planning. Event managers are now more prepared to adapt to sudden changes, whether it's a health crisis, a natural disaster, or another unforeseen event. This resilience will be crucial in navigating the uncertainties of the future.

Evolving Attendee Expectations: The pandemic has also transformed attendee expectations. Participants now seek more value and flexibility from the events they choose to attend. They expect seamless virtual experiences, meaningful in-person interactions and content that is highly relevant to their needs. Personalisation and convenience have become key drivers of attendee satisfaction.

For instance, many attendees now expect on-demand access to event content, allowing them to engage at their own pace. They also value opportunities for interactive engagement, whether through live Q&A sessions, networking platforms, or virtual meetups. As the industry continues to evolve, meeting these expectations will be critical to the success of future events.

Strategic Resilience Planning: Looking ahead, event managers must develop long-term resilience strategies. This involves diversifying revenue streams, such as offering premium online content or creating membership-based event series, to ensure financial stability in the face of future disruptions. It also includes planning for adaptable event models that can quickly pivot between in-person, virtual and hybrid formats as needed.

Hybrid and Virtual Events: The Growing Importance of Technology in Event Participation

Technology has always played a vital role in event management, but its importance has been magnified in the post-pandemic era. Hybrid and virtual events are at the forefront of this technological revolution, offering new possibilities for participation, engagement and content delivery.

The Hybrid Event Model: Hybrid events, which combine physical and digital experiences, have become a cornerstone of modern event strategy. This model allows organisers to reach a wider audience by catering to both in-person attendees and those participating remotely. The flexibility of hybrid events means that participants can choose the format that best suits their needs, whether they prefer the networking opportunities of an in-person event or the convenience of a virtual one.

The success of hybrid events hinges on the seamless integration of technology. High-quality streaming, interactive platforms and robust digital infrastructure are essential to creating a cohesive experience for all attendees. For instance, live polls, virtual breakout rooms and real-time chat functions can help bridge the gap between in-person and remote participants, fostering a sense of community regardless of physical location.

Virtual Events: Beyond the Pandemic Virtual events, which gained prominence during the pandemic, are set to continue as a key component of the event landscape. While they may not fully replace in-person events, virtual events offer distinct advantages, including lower costs, greater accessibility and reduced environmental impact.

Virtual platforms have become increasingly sophisticated, offering a range of features that enhance the attendee experience. From AI-powered networking tools that match participants based on their interests to immersive virtual environments that replicate the feel of a physical venue, the possibilities for innovation are vast. Additionally, virtual events can be recorded and repurposed, extending their value beyond the live experience.

Cybersecurity and Data Privacy: As events move increasingly online, cybersecurity and data privacy have become critical concerns. Event managers must ensure that the platforms they use are secure and that attendee data is protected from breaches. This involves implementing robust cybersecurity measures, such as encryption, secure payment processing and regular security audits.

Additionally, transparency about how attendee data is collected, stored and used is essential for building trust. Event managers should communicate clearly with participants about data privacy policies and provide options for attendees to control their data.

Challenges and Opportunities: While hybrid and virtual events offer many benefits, they also present unique challenges. Ensuring engagement in a virtual environment can be difficult, as attendees may be more easily distracted or disconnected from the content. To overcome this, organisers need to be creative in their approach, using interactive elements, personalised content and engaging visuals to capture and retain attention.

Moreover, the shift to digital platforms requires investment in technology and training. Event managers must be proficient in using digital tools and platforms and they need to stay abreast of the latest technological advancements to deliver high-quality experiences. The rise of hybrid and virtual events also opens up opportunities for collaboration with tech companies, creating new avenues for innovation and growth in the industry.

The Economic Contribution of Events: A Deep Dive into the Value Events Bring to the Economy

The events industry is not just a driver of social and cultural engagement; it also plays a significant role in the global economy. Events generate revenue, create jobs and stimulate growth across various sectors, making them a vital component of economic development. In this section, we will explore the economic impact of events, with a particular focus on the UK and the broader global context.

The UK Events Industry: In the UK, the events industry is a major contributor to the economy, supporting a wide range of industries, including hospitality, tourism and transportation. According to a report by the Business Visits & Events Partnership (BVEP), the UK events industry was valued at approximately £70 billion in 2019, before the pandemic. This figure reflects the direct and indirect economic benefits generated by events, from spending on venues and accommodations to the ripple effects on local businesses.

Events also play a crucial role in promoting the UK as a global destination for business and leisure. International conferences, trade shows and cultural festivals attract visitors from around the world, boosting tourism and enhancing the country's international reputation. The government's recognition of the value of events is evident in its support for the industry, including initiatives to attract major global events to the UK.

Global Economic Impact: On a global scale, the events industry is a powerhouse of economic activity. The International Congress and Convention Association (ICCA) estimates that the global meetings industry generates over $1 trillion in direct spending annually. This spending encompasses a wide range of activities, from event planning and execution to attendee expenditures on travel, accommodation and dining.

In addition to direct spending, events contribute to economic development by fostering innovation, driving trade and facilitating knowledge exchange. Conferences and trade shows, for example, provide a platform for businesses to showcase new products, enter new markets and establish strategic partnerships. Cultural and entertainment events, meanwhile, generate revenue through ticket sales, sponsorships and media rights, while also promoting cultural exchange and social cohesion.

Long-Term Economic Benefits: The economic impact of events extends beyond the immediate revenue generated. Events can have long-term benefits for the host cities and countries, including increased tourism, infrastructure development and enhanced global visibility. For example, hosting a major international event, such as the Olympics or the World Expo, can lead to significant investments in infrastructure, from transportation networks to sports facilities, which continue to benefit the local economy long after the event has concluded.

Moreover, events can serve as catalysts for urban regeneration and economic revitalisation. The development of new event venues, hotels and entertainment districts can transform underutilised areas into vibrant economic hubs, attracting businesses and residents and driving long-term growth.

Sustainability and Economic Impact: As the events industry continues to evolve, sustainability has become a critical factor in its economic contribution. Sustainable events not only reduce environmental impact but also create long-term economic benefits. For example, events that prioritise local sourcing, waste reduction and energy efficiency can lower operational costs and attract environmentally conscious sponsors and attendees.

Additionally, the growing emphasis on Corporate Social Responsibility (CSR) within the events industry can enhance its economic impact. By aligning events with broader social and environmental goals, organisers can create value for communities, foster social goodwill and strengthen the reputation of their brands. This approach not only contributes to economic growth but also ensures that events are aligned with the values and expectations of modern society.

The Role of Data Analytics and AI in Shaping the Future of Events

As we look to the future, data analytics and artificial intelligence (AI) will play an increasingly important role in event management. These technologies offer powerful tools for understanding attendee behaviour, personalising experiences and optimising event outcomes.

Data-Driven Decision Making: Data analytics allows event managers to gather insights into attendee preferences, engagement levels and feedback. By analysing this data, organisers can make informed decisions about content, format and logistics, ensuring that events are tailored to the needs and expectations of their audience.

For example, analysing data from previous events can help identify trends in attendee behaviour, such as which sessions were most popular, or which networking opportunities were most effective. This information can then be used to design future events that are more engaging and impactful.

AI-Powered Personalisation: AI is revolutionising the way events are personalised. Through machine learning algorithms, AI can analyse vast amounts of data to provide personalised recommendations for attendees, such as suggesting sessions, networking opportunities, or content based on their interests and behaviour.

For instance, an AI-powered event app could recommend specific sessions or exhibitors to an attendee based on their past interactions, enhancing the overall experience. AI can also be used to automate tasks such as registration, scheduling and follow-up, freeing up event managers to focus on more strategic aspects of the event.

Predictive Analytics: Predictive analytics, a subset of AI, can be used to anticipate trends and outcomes, helping event managers to plan more effectively. By analysing historical data, predictive models can forecast attendance, engagement levels and even potential challenges, allowing organisers to proactively address issues before they arise.

For example, predictive analytics can help determine the optimal time to send out invitations or launch marketing campaigns based on past attendee responses. This ensures that outreach efforts are timely and effective, maximising the chances of a successful event.

Cybersecurity: Protecting Event Data in the Digital Age

As events increasingly rely on digital platforms, cybersecurity has become a critical concern. Protecting attendee data, ensuring secure transactions and safeguarding against cyber threats are essential components of modern event management.

Data Protection and Privacy: With the rise of virtual and hybrid events, more attendee data is being collected than ever before. This includes personal information, payment details and behavioural data. Event managers must ensure that this data is protected in accordance with data privacy regulations, such as the General Data Protection Regulation (GDPR) in the UK and EU.

This involves implementing robust security measures, such as encryption, secure servers and regular security audits. Additionally, transparency about how data is collected, stored and used is crucial for building trust with attendees. Providing clear privacy policies and giving attendees control over their data can help ensure compliance and foster confidence.

Cybersecurity Best Practices: To protect against cyber threats, event managers should adopt best practices in cybersecurity. This includes securing all digital platforms used for registration, payment processing and virtual participation. Multi-factor authentication, firewalls and regular software updates are essential for preventing breaches.

In addition, event managers should be prepared to respond quickly to any security incidents. This includes having a clear incident response plan in place, training staff on cybersecurity protocols and regularly testing the security of digital systems.

The Future of Cybersecurity in Events: As the digital landscape continues to evolve, cybersecurity will remain a top priority for event managers. Emerging technologies, such as blockchain, may offer new ways to enhance security and protect data. By staying informed about the latest developments in cybersecurity and continuously improving security measures, event managers can ensure that their events are safe, secure and trusted by all participants.

Chapter Summary

The future of events is being shaped by profound changes in technology, attendee expectations and the global economy. As event professionals, it is essential to embrace these changes, leverage new technologies and continue to deliver experiences that inspire, engage and drive meaningful outcomes.

From the lasting impact of the pandemic to the rise of hybrid and virtual events, the future of events will be defined by innovation, resilience and adaptability. By staying ahead of trends and focusing on data-driven decision making, cybersecurity and sustainability, event managers can create successful events that contribute to the economy, meet the evolving needs of attendees and set new standards for excellence in the industry.

As we conclude this chapter, remember that the most successful events are those that not only respond to current trends but also anticipate the needs and desires of tomorrow's participants. By maintaining a strategic focus and continually evolving, the events industry will continue to be a driving force for social, cultural and economic development in the years to come.

In Conclusion: Your Role in the Meeting Economy

As we bring this exploration of event management to a close, it is clear that the role of event professionals extends far beyond the logistics of planning and executing gatherings. Event management is a discipline that stands at the intersection of strategy, creativity and leadership, influencing industries, economies and societies in profound ways. It is time to recognise event management as a distinct discipline, one that requires a unique blend of skills and a deep understanding of human connection, business objectives and global trends.

Becoming a Strategic Player: Building Your Influence and Impact in the Events Industry

In the evolving landscape of event management, your role as an event professional is more critical than ever. You are not just organising events; you are orchestrating experiences that shape perceptions, foster relationships and drive economic growth. As a strategic player in the meeting economy, your influence extends across industries and borders, making you an invaluable asset to any organisation.

To continue building your influence, it's essential to position yourself as a thought leader in the field. This involves staying ahead of industry trends, continuously enhancing your skills and actively contributing to the broader conversation about the future of events. Engage with professional networks, attend industry conferences and share your insights through writing, speaking, or teaching. By doing so, you not only elevate your own career but also contribute to the advancement of the entire profession.

As an event professional, you are also a connector of people, ideas and opportunities. Your ability to bring the right people together at the right time can have a lasting impact on businesses and communities. Embrace this role with the understanding that every event you manage is an opportunity to create value, build relationships and leave a legacy that extends far beyond the event itself.

The Power of Presence: The Long-Term Benefits of Active Participation in Events

Active participation in events is a powerful tool for building and maintaining your presence in the industry. Whether you are organising or attending, your presence at events positions you as a key player in the meeting economy. It allows you to stay connected with industry trends, expand your professional network and continuously learn from others in the field.

The power of presence goes beyond just showing up. It's about being fully engaged; listening, contributing and making meaningful connections. This active participation not only enhances your own professional development but also strengthens the events you are involved in. By bringing your insights, experience and enthusiasm to the table, you contribute to the richness of the event and help create an environment where ideas can flourish and partnerships can thrive.

Moreover, your presence at events serves as a reminder of the importance of human connection in a digital world. While technology has transformed the way we communicate, the value of face-to-face interaction remains unparalleled. Events provide a space where relationships are built, trust is established and collaboration is fostered. As an event professional, your role in facilitating these interactions is crucial and your active participation is a testament to the enduring power of human connection.

The Legacy of Events: Creating Lasting Economic, Social and Cultural Value

The true impact of events is measured not just by the immediate success of the gathering but by the lasting legacy it leaves behind. Well-designed events have the power to create significant economic, social and cultural value, shaping communities and industries for years to come. As an event professional, you are the architect of these legacies and your work has a profound ripple effect on the world around you.

Economically, events drive growth by generating revenue, creating jobs and stimulating local businesses. They attract visitors, foster trade and promote investment in infrastructure. Culturally, events serve as platforms for the exchange of ideas, the celebration of diversity and the promotion of local heritage. Socially, events bring people together, build communities and create spaces for dialogue and understanding.

As ambassadors of industries and localities, event professionals play a pivotal role in showcasing what a region or sector has to offer. You are the gateway through which visitors and participants experience the best of what a place or industry has to offer. This role comes with great responsibility, as your work not only reflects the event but also the broader community it represents.

Given the strategic importance of events, it is imperative that event professionals be recognised accordingly by relevant bodies. This includes formal recognition of event management as a distinct discipline, with established standards, certifications and career pathways. Event professionals should be acknowledged for their expertise in not only logistics but also in strategy, marketing, risk management and human relations. This recognition will not only elevate the profession but also ensure that those who dedicate their careers to this field are equipped with the resources and support they need to succeed.

Conclusion: Shaping the Future of the Meeting Economy

As we look to the future, the role of event professionals will continue to grow in importance. The meeting economy is not just about bringing people together; it is about creating opportunities, driving innovation and fostering sustainable growth. By embracing your role as a strategic player, actively participating in events and focusing on the long-term impact of your work, you can help shape the future of this vital industry.

The legacy you leave as an event professional goes far beyond the events you organise. It is embedded in the relationships you foster, the value you create and the communities you build. By recognising event management as a distinct discipline and acknowledging the critical role of event professionals, we can ensure that this legacy continues to thrive, creating a better, more connected world for generations to come.

Appendices

Appendix A: The Event Engagement Model (EEM)

Overview: The Event Engagement Model (EEM) is designed to maximise participant engagement and outcomes at events. It focuses on three key stages: Pre-Event Engagement, On-Site Engagement and Post-Event Engagement. By strategically planning and executing activities at each stage, event professionals can ensure that participants are fully engaged and derive maximum value from the event.

Stages and Components:

1. **Pre-Event Engagement:**
    - **Research & Identification:** Identify key sessions, speakers and attendees aligned with your goals.
    - **Goal Setting:** Set Specific, Measurable, Achievable, Relevant and Time-bound (SMART) goals for the event.
    - **Pitch Preparation:** Prepare a tailored pitch to introduce yourself effectively at the event.
2. **On-Site Engagement:**
    - **Session Participation:** Actively engage in sessions through questions, discussions and social media.
    - **Networking Strategy:** Focus on meaningful interactions and use networking tools to connect with key contacts.

- **Real-Time Social Engagement:** Share insights and connect with other participants through event hashtags and apps.

3. **Post-Event Engagement:**
    - **Structured Follow-Up:** Send personalised follow-up messages, referencing conversations and proposing next steps.
    - **Content Sharing & Value Addition:** Share relevant content and maintain regular engagement with new contacts.
    - **Long-Term Engagement Strategy:** Schedule regular check-ins to maintain and deepen relationships.

Application: This model provides a structured approach to engagement that can be customised to different events and objectives. By following the EEM, participants can enhance their networking, learning and overall event experience.

EVENT ENGAGEMENT MODEL (EEM)

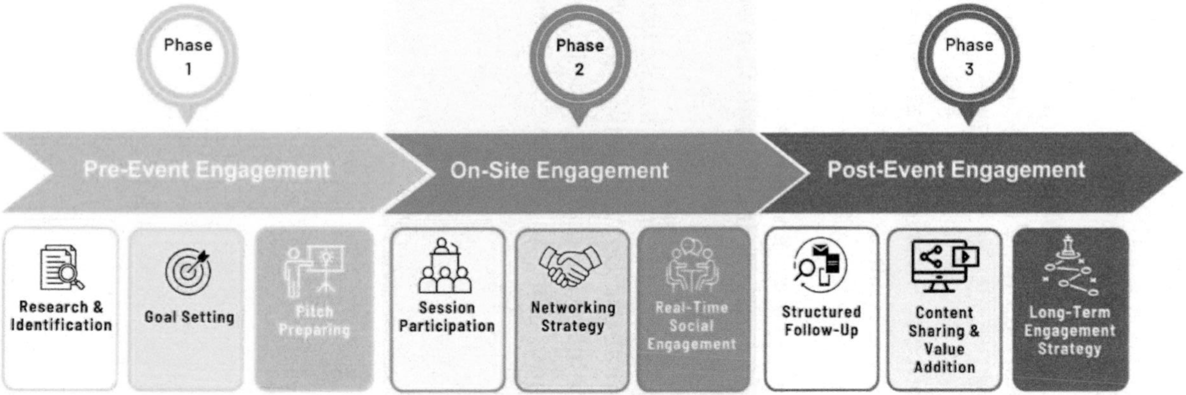

Phase 1

Pre-Event Engagement

Research & Identification

Goal Setting

Pitch Preparing

Phase 2

On-Site Engagement

Session Participation

Networking Strategy

Real-Time Social Engagement

Phase 3

Post-Event Engagement

Structured Follow-Up

Content Sharing & Value Addition

Long-Term Engagement Strategy

Appendix B: Global Connection Framework

Overview: The Global Connection Framework is a comprehensive suite of tools, resources and services designed to help organisations establish, manage and optimise global partnerships. It aligns with the United Nations Sustainable Development Goal 17 (SDG 17): Partnerships for the Goals.

Framework Components:

1. **Strategic Partnership Development Guide:** Offers guidance on building and nurturing partnerships aligned with organisational goals.

2. **Collaborative Technology Platform:** Facilitates seamless communication and collaboration across borders.

3. **Capacity Building and Training Programs:** Enhances skills and capabilities needed for sustaining global partnerships.

4. **Monitoring and Evaluation Tools:** Tracks the performance and impact of partnerships to ensure they deliver value.

5. **Consulting and Advisory Services:** Provides expert guidance on navigating and optimising global partnerships.

Application: This framework serves as a strategic resource for organisations looking to expand their global reach and build sustainable partnerships. Each component is designed to address specific aspects of partnership development and management.

GLOBAL CONNECTION FRAMEWORK

Appendix C: Stakeholder Satisfaction Measurement Framework (SSMF)

Overview: The Stakeholder Satisfaction Measurement Framework (SSMF) provides a structured approach to assessing and improving stakeholder satisfaction. It is divided into four key stages: Identification, Data Collection, Analysis and Action Planning.

Stages and Components:

1. **Identification:**
    - **Stakeholder Mapping:** Identify all relevant stakeholders and their expectations.
    - **Expectation Setting:** Determine and document the specific needs of each stakeholder group.
2. **Data Collection:**
    - **Surveys and Feedback Forms:** Gather quantitative and qualitative feedback from stakeholders.
    - **Interviews and Focus Groups:** Conduct in-depth discussions to gain deeper insights.
    - **Observation and Behavioural Data:** Monitor stakeholder interactions during the event.
3. **Analysis:**
    - **Quantitative Analysis:** Analyse survey data to identify trends and satisfaction levels.
    - **Qualitative Analysis:** Review feedback for recurring themes and actionable insights.
    - **Benchmarking:** Compare satisfaction data against industry standards or past events.

4. **Action Planning:**
    - **Stakeholder Engagement Plan:** Develop strategies to address concerns and improve satisfaction.
    - **Continuous Improvement Loop:** Regularly update and refine engagement strategies based on feedback.
    - **Reporting and Communication:** Share results and planned improvements with stakeholders.

Application: The SSMF enables event managers to systematically evaluate stakeholder satisfaction and implement strategies to enhance future events. By continuously monitoring and improving stakeholder relationships, event professionals can ensure long-term success and loyalty.

Stakeholder Satisfaction Measurement Framework (SSMF)

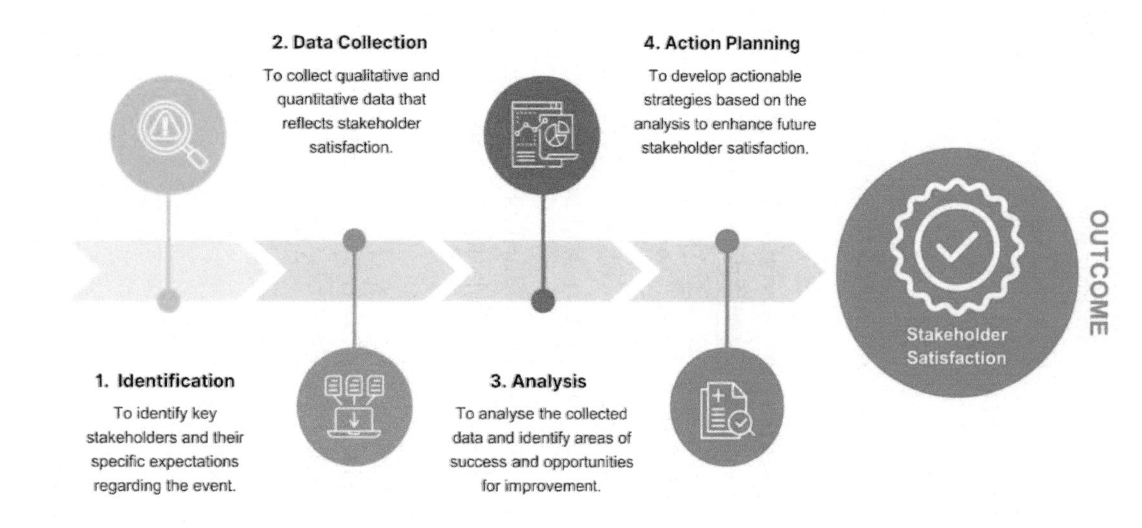

Appendix D: Crisis Management Framework

Overview: The Crisis Management Framework is a strategic tool designed to help event professionals prepare for, respond to and recover from crises. It is divided into four key phases: Mitigation, Preparedness, Response and Recovery.

Phases and Components:

1. **Mitigation:**
   - **Risk Assessment:** Identify potential risks and vulnerabilities.
   - **Preventative Measures:** Implement strategies to minimise identified risks.
2. **Preparedness:**
   - **Crisis Planning:** Develop detailed crisis management plans and protocols.
   - **Training and Drills:** Conduct regular training sessions and simulations to prepare staff.
3. **Response:**
   - **Crisis Activation:** Implement the crisis plan when an incident occurs.
   - **Communication Management:** Ensure clear, consistent communication with stakeholders during the crisis.
4. **Recovery:**
   - **Post-Crisis Review:** Analyse the crisis response to identify successes and areas for improvement.

- **Rebuilding Trust:** Implement strategies to restore stakeholder confidence and reputation.

Application: The Crisis Management Framework equips event professionals with the tools and strategies needed to effectively manage crises. By following this framework, events can be safeguarded against disruptions, ensuring continuity and protecting the organisation's reputation.

CRISIS MANAGEMENT FRAMEWORK
(CMF)
1. Mitigation
Conduct risk assessments, identify potential risks, implement preventive measures.
2. Preparedness
Develop detailed crisis management plans, train staff, establish communication protocols, conduct crisis drills.
3. Response
Activate crisis management team, communicate with stakeholders, execute contingency plans, manage real-time decisions.
4. Recovery
Assess the impact, restore normal operations, conduct post-crisis analysis, refine crisis management plans.

Appendix E: Metrics for Measuring Event Success

Overview: Measuring the success of an event is critical for understanding its impact and value. This appendix presents a comprehensive set of metrics that event professionals can use to evaluate different aspects of an event.

Key Metrics:

1. **Attendance Metrics:**
   - **Registration vs. Attendance:** Compare the number of registrations with actual attendance.
   - **Demographic Breakdown:** Analyse the demographics of attendees to assess reach and relevance.
2. **Engagement Metrics:**
   - **Session Attendance:** Track the number of participants in each session.
   - **Interaction Levels:** Measure engagement through Q&A participation, polls and social media activity.
3. **Satisfaction Metrics:**
   - **Post-Event Surveys:** Gauge attendee satisfaction through feedback on content, logistics and overall experience.
   - **Net Promoter Score (NPS):** Assess the likelihood of attendees recommending the event to others.
4. **ROI Metrics:**

- **Revenue Generated:** Calculate total revenue from ticket sales, sponsorships and other sources.
- **Cost vs. Benefit:** Evaluate the financial return on investment by comparing costs with generated revenue.

5. **Impact Metrics:**
   - **Long-Term Outcomes:** Assess the long-term impact of the event on business objectives, such as lead generation, partnerships and brand awareness.
   - **Sustainability Metrics:** Measure the environmental and social impact of the event, including waste reduction and community engagement.

Application: These metrics provide a comprehensive framework for evaluating the success of events. By systematically tracking and analysing these metrics, event professionals can gain valuable insights into what worked well and where improvements are needed, ensuring continuous growth and success.

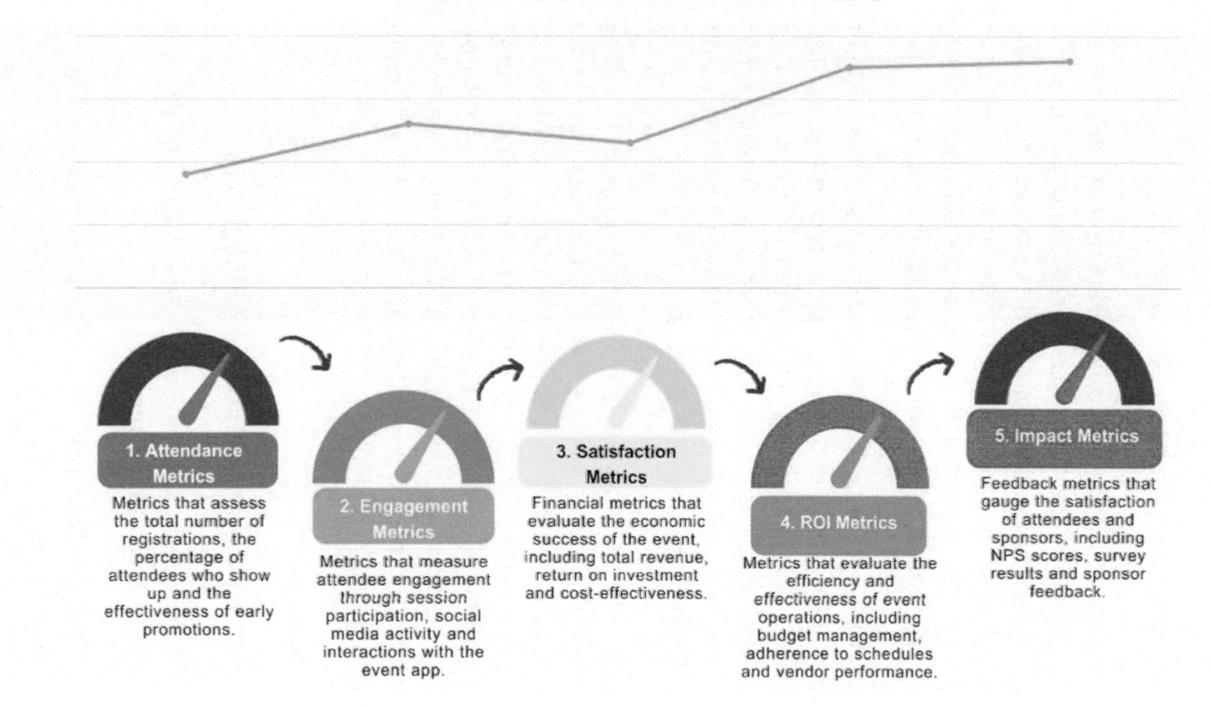
EVENT SUCCESS METRICS
1. Attendance Metrics
Metrics that assess the total number of registrations, the percentage of attendees who show up and the effectiveness of early promotions.
2. Engagement Metrics
Metrics that measure attendee engagement through session participation, social media activity and interactions with the event app.
3. Satisfaction Metrics
Financial metrics that evaluate the economic success of the event, including total revenue, return on investment and cost-effectiveness.
4. ROI Metrics
Metrics that evaluate the efficiency and effectiveness of event operations, including budget management, adherence to schedules and vendor performance.
5. Impact Metrics
Feedback metrics that gauge the satisfaction of attendees and sponsors, including NPS scores, survey results and sponsor feedback.

Case Studies

Introduction to the Case Studies

Strategic meetings and events often reveal their true value through real-life examples. Case studies provide a clear lens into the challenges, solutions and successes that shape high-level events. They demonstrate how strategies evolve in response to changing circumstances and how solutions are implemented to deliver measurable outcomes.

This section presents five detailed case studies, reflecting the principles and frameworks discussed in the earlier chapters. Each case study showcases an event that I have had the privilege of managing, from crisis management in global summits to success in virtual environments and facilitating strategic partnerships.

Through these examples, you will see how critical strategies such as stakeholder engagement, crisis management and measuring event outcomes were applied to achieve significant results. These are not theoretical concepts but tested methodologies that have delivered real business value, including securing multi-million-pound investments and managing the complexities of international events during a global pandemic.

What to Expect

Each case study is structured to highlight:

- **The Event Overview**: A description of the event's objectives and context.
- **The Challenges**: Key obstacles faced while executing the event.

- **The Solutions Implemented**: The strategic approaches and frameworks applied to address those challenges.
- **The Outcomes**: The measurable results achieved, from partnerships to investments and stakeholder satisfaction.
- **Lessons Learned**: Key takeaways that can be applied to future events.

Why Case Studies Matter Successful outcomes in event management are often the result of proven strategies and thoughtful execution. The case studies in this section offer practical insights into navigating the uncertainties of event planning while meeting stakeholder objectives. Whether handling a global crisis or transitioning to a virtual platform, these examples show how even the most challenging events can be delivered with impactful results.

As you explore these cases, consider how the frameworks and strategies discussed earlier can be adapted to your own events. Whether you are organising an investment summit or managing a virtual conference, the insights shared here will provide both guidance and inspiration for your future success.

Case Study 1: Crisis Management in Events

Event Overview

The **Africa-Dubai Investment Business Summit** was designed to bring together key stakeholders from Africa and the UAE, including government officials, investors and business leaders, to facilitate trade and investment partnerships. The summit aimed to address sectors such as infrastructure, technology and energy, with a strong focus on fostering cross-border business deals. However, just days before the event, the UAE imposed sudden travel restrictions on several African countries, which affected approximately 30% of the registered participants, including major sponsors, delegates and speakers.

Challenges:
The sudden travel restrictions created an immediate challenge: how to proceed with an in-person event when a significant portion of participants could no longer attend. The event risked losing engagement from key stakeholders, sponsors and attendees, who were now unable to participate physically. The challenge was to restructure the event in a way that ensured its success while maintaining strong relationships with those who could no longer attend in person.

Solutions Implemented:
To overcome the crisis, the event was adapted to accommodate both in-person and virtual participants, with a revised agenda and a more intimate setup. Key strategies included:

- **Live Streaming Portal for Virtual Engagement:**
  A live streaming portal was quickly deployed to enable virtual engagement for the 30% of participants who were affected by the travel restrictions. This ensured that they could still access keynote speeches, panel

discussions and key sessions in real time, while also participating remotely in some aspects of the event.

- **Agenda Restructure:**
  The event agenda was updated to include a conference format featuring keynote addresses, panel discussions and pitches, followed by a more intimate **roundtable session** and **B2B meetings**. This allowed the in-person attendees to have more focused, high-quality interactions while maintaining engagement with the virtual participants.
- **Enhanced Stakeholder Experience:**
  The smaller, in-person group allowed for a more personalised experience. Sponsors and stakeholders who were present had greater access to key decision-makers in the room and the roundtable sessions created an environment for more in-depth discussions.
- **Ongoing Communication:**
  Regular communication with both in-person and virtual participants was maintained. Those who couldn't attend physically were kept informed of how they could still participate via the live stream and virtual engagement tools.

Outcomes:
Despite the travel restrictions, the **Africa-Dubai Investment Business Summit** succeeded in achieving its primary goals. Key outcomes included:

- **Hybrid event success:** Although 30% of participants were unable to attend in person, the live streaming portal allowed for remote engagement. Over **70% of virtual participants** accessed the live stream and provided positive feedback on the content and accessibility.

- **In-person networking and deals:** The revised agenda created a more intimate setting, leading to deeper engagement among the in-person attendees. Several high-level partnerships were initiated during the B2B meetings, with follow-up discussions planned post-event.

- **Sponsor satisfaction:** Sponsors appreciated the flexibility of the revised format, which allowed them to maintain visibility both on-site and through the virtual platform. **80% of sponsors** expressed satisfaction with their involvement and several confirmed interest in future participation.

Lessons Learned:
This experience highlighted the importance of **flexibility and adaptability** in event management. Even when external factors such as travel restrictions disrupt an event, a well-thought-out crisis management plan can allow the event to proceed successfully. Providing hybrid solutions such as live streaming options for virtual engagement and restructuring the agenda to suit the circumstances ensured that the event continued to deliver value to all participants.

Case Study 2: Building Partnerships through Strategic Networking

Event Overview

The **UK-Nigeria Investment Showcase** was designed to create a platform for fostering new business opportunities and partnerships between UK investors and Nigerian businesses. It focused on sectors with high potential for growth, such as energy, technology, agriculture and infrastructure, aligning with the goal of driving economic collaboration and investment.

Challenges

Several challenges emerged when facilitating meaningful connections between diverse stakeholders:

- **Different Investment Priorities**: Investors from the UK and businesses from Nigeria had varying objectives and expectations, making it difficult to identify mutual interests quickly.
- **Cross-Cultural Communication**: Navigating cultural nuances and business practices between the two countries presented potential barriers to effective networking.
- **Ensuring Productive Interactions**: The success of the event depended on creating an environment where valuable interactions could happen, leading to long-term business partnerships rather than surface-level introductions.

Solutions Implemented

To overcome these challenges, a combination of structured networking and personalised engagement strategies was employed:

- **Curated Networking Sessions**: By utilising insights from the **Global Connection Framework**, pre-event research identified key stakeholders with complementary goals. Attendees were paired strategically, ensuring that networking sessions were focused on real opportunities for collaboration.
- **Facilitated Introductions**: To mitigate potential cross-cultural barriers, sessions were supported by expert facilitators familiar with both UK and Nigerian markets. This ensured that participants could communicate effectively and align their business goals more seamlessly.
- **Targeted Roundtables**: Specialised roundtable discussions were organised to align industry leaders with high-potential business opportunities. These focused on key investment sectors and featured structured agendas to maximise the time for meaningful conversations.

Outcomes

The event was highly successful in achieving its objectives:

- **Partnerships and Trade Agreements**: The UK-Nigeria Investment Showcase resulted in several significant trade agreements and business partnerships, particularly in the energy and technology sectors. Attendees highlighted the event as a key turning point in developing their business strategies.
- **New Investment Deals**: Multiple UK investors reported that the showcase allowed them to discover new opportunities in Nigeria's emerging markets,

leading to several multi-million-pound investment deals.

- **Enhanced Economic Ties**: The showcase contributed to strengthening the bilateral relationship between the UK and Nigeria, fostering long-term economic collaboration.

Lessons Learned

1. **Pre-event Research is Critical**: Understanding stakeholder priorities beforehand allowed for more meaningful and productive networking sessions.
2. **Cultural Sensitivity Enhances Engagement**: Addressing cultural differences through facilitated communication helped build trust and opened the door for more substantive conversations.
3. **Strategic Networking Yields Results**: When networking is structured and goal-driven, it leads to tangible outcomes such as partnerships, investments and long-term collaboration.

Case Study 3: Delivering Stakeholder Satisfaction

Event Overview

The **International Produced Water Management Conference and Exhibition** was originally scheduled to take place over two days in Lagos. The event aimed to bring together industry leaders in the oil and gas sector to discuss solutions for managing produced water, showcasing technologies and fostering collaboration.

However, as the Covid-19 pandemic caused global lockdowns, it became impossible to hold the in-person event. Rather than postponing, I recommended moving the entire event to a virtual format. After several stakeholder meetings, this plan was agreed upon and the event was redesigned for a digital environment.

Challenges

The transition from an in-person event to a virtual one during the pandemic introduced several challenges:

- **Complete Event Redesign**: The event had to be quickly restructured to fit a virtual format, including new platforms, schedules and engagement strategies.
- **Nullifying On-Ground Contracts**: Contracts with on-ground suppliers were voided and new contracts had to be established with virtual platform providers.
- **Convincing Sponsors to Continue**: One of the most difficult tasks was persuading sponsors that the virtual event would still provide value and deliver the desired impact in terms of visibility and engagement.

Solutions Implemented

To manage these challenges, the following solutions were implemented:

- **Virtual Event Transformation**: The event was redesigned to suit a virtual platform, with digital exhibition booths, live-streamed keynotes and interactive breakout sessions. The experience was crafted to simulate the original event's networking opportunities and audience engagement.
- **Proactive Stakeholder Engagement**: Regular updates and virtual platform demonstrations were conducted with sponsors, exhibitors and attendees to keep them informed about the new structure. Stakeholders were reengaged with clear demonstrations of how the virtual format could meet their needs.
- **Contract Adjustments**: All on-ground contracts were swiftly nullified and new agreements were made with virtual providers, ensuring the event could still deliver quality and value to all participants.
- **Sponsor Reassurance**: A key challenge was convincing sponsors to stay on board. The strategy involved presenting metrics and engagement potential of virtual events, demonstrating that they could still reach their target audience effectively, despite the format change.

Outcomes

Despite the pandemic and the significant format shift, the event was a success:

- **High Stakeholder Satisfaction**: Sponsors, exhibitors and attendees were pleased with the outcome, with many commenting on the seamless transition to the virtual format. Sponsors especially appreciated the wider reach that the virtual event provided.

- **Expanded Participation**: The virtual format attracted more participants than initially expected, as the digital nature allowed attendees from various locations to join without travel restrictions.
- **Sponsor Retention**: Despite initial hesitation, all major sponsors remained engaged, with several extending their sponsorships to future events after seeing the potential of the virtual platform.

Lessons Learned

1. **Adaptability During Crisis**: The swift pivot from a physical to a virtual event during the pandemic highlights the importance of flexibility and innovation in event management.
2. **Effective Communication**: Constant, clear communication with stakeholders built the confidence necessary to ensure their continued support.
3. **Virtual Formats Offer New Opportunities**: Virtual events, when executed strategically, can offer unique advantages such as increased participation and global reach, making them a valuable tool even beyond the pandemic context.

Case Study 4: Managing a Virtual Event

Event Overview

The **UK-Africa FinTech Summit** was a two-day virtual event aimed at connecting fintech leaders, investors and innovators from the UK and Africa. The event's objective was to foster collaboration between financial technology companies, investors and government bodies, while exploring opportunities to drive financial inclusion across the African continent. The summit featured keynote presentations, panel discussions and virtual networking sessions.

Due to the nature of the summit and the ongoing global pandemic, the event was planned entirely as a virtual experience, marking a significant shift from the traditional in-person model.

Challenges

Several challenges arose in managing this fully virtual event:

- **Participant Engagement**: One of the key concerns was maintaining high levels of engagement in a virtual setting. Virtual events can sometimes lack the immersive experience of physical ones, making it more challenging to keep participants engaged throughout.
- **Facilitating Networking**: One of the primary goals of the event was to encourage networking among fintech leaders and investors. Achieving meaningful networking in a virtual environment can be complex, especially without physical interactions.
- **Technical Reliability**: Given the scale of the event and the number of participants joining from multiple

countries, ensuring technical stability and managing any potential disruptions were crucial concerns.

Solutions Implemented

To address these challenges, a combination of innovative strategies and technology was employed:

- **Interactive Sessions**: The event design included highly interactive sessions to ensure participant engagement. Polls, live Q&A segments and breakout discussions were incorporated into the agenda to encourage audience participation and create a sense of interaction throughout.
- **Virtual Networking Tools**: Specialised virtual networking platforms were used to facilitate meaningful interactions. These tools allowed participants to connect via one-on-one video meetings, join thematic group discussions and schedule follow-up meetings during and after the summit. This helped replicate the networking dynamics of an in-person event.
- **Pre-event Technical Rehearsals**: A series of rehearsals were conducted with speakers, panellists and moderators to test the technical setup and ensure familiarity with the virtual platform. This minimised the risk of technical issues during the live event.
- **Real-time Tech Support**: A dedicated tech support team was on standby throughout the event to troubleshoot any technical difficulties faced by participants, ensuring minimal disruption.

Outcomes

The virtual UK-Africa FinTech Summit was a resounding success:

- **Increased Participation**: The virtual format allowed for greater global participation, with attendees joining from across Africa, the UK and beyond. The flexibility of the virtual setting attracted a larger and more diverse audience than originally anticipated.
- **Engagement Metrics**: Polls, live Q&A sessions and virtual networking sessions saw high participation rates. Feedback surveys highlighted the interactive features as key elements that kept the audience engaged.
- **Successful Networking**: Despite the lack of physical interactions, many attendees were able to connect with new business partners and investors through the virtual networking tools. Post-event follow-ups indicated that several participants were able to establish valuable partnerships.

Lessons Learned

1. **Virtual Events Can Drive Global Participation**: A virtual format opens up opportunities for a wider audience, allowing for more inclusivity and global reach.
2. **Engagement Requires Interactivity**: Keeping virtual audiences engaged requires careful planning and the use of interactive tools such as polls, Q&A sessions and breakout discussions.
3. **Technical Preparedness is Key**: Pre-event rehearsals and real-time technical support are essential for ensuring a smooth and successful virtual event.

Case Study 5: Measuring Event Success

Event Overview

The **Empower Gala** was a prestigious event aimed at celebrating culture, achievement and the diversity of Kent. Designed as a high-level social gathering, it brought together influential leaders from the Public, Private and Charity sectors across the region. The gala's inclusive atmosphere was amplified by the unique dress code, **"Fashion of Wakanda,"** which embraced and celebrated the richness of cultural heritage while symbolising global diversity and unity.

The primary goal was to recognise and celebrate the achievements of Kent's most notable individuals and organisations, while fostering cross-sector and cross-cultural collaboration. Measuring the success of the gala went beyond tracking attendance; it required assessing how well the event facilitated connections across sectors and celebrated the diverse cultures represented in Kent.

Challenges

The event presented several challenges to ensure it achieved its objectives:

- **Defining Success in a Diverse Social Setting**: While the gala was celebratory in nature, it needed to generate meaningful outcomes in terms of relationship-building, especially in a context that embraced cultural diversity.
- **Engaging a Diverse Audience**: The gala attracted a broad spectrum of attendees from various sectors and cultural backgrounds. This required careful planning to ensure that the evening encouraged

collaboration, cultural appreciation and engagement among these groups.

- **Tracking Cross-Sector and Cross-Cultural Engagement**: Measuring the success of the event meant evaluating how effectively it brought together leaders from diverse cultural and professional backgrounds to foster future partnerships.

Solutions Implemented

To ensure the gala met its goals of fostering both cross-sector and cross-cultural engagement, the following strategies were employed:

- **Focused Networking Opportunities**: Specialised networking zones were created to encourage interaction between attendees from different sectors and cultural backgrounds. By promoting collaboration through interactive moments, the event successfully fostered connections across diverse groups.

- **Inclusive Theme and Atmosphere**: The "Fashion of Wakanda" theme brought excitement and also served as a powerful celebration of global cultures. It encouraged attendees to express their heritage, fostering an inclusive and celebratory environment that honoured diversity in all its forms.

- **Cultural Representation**: The gala's programme featured cultural elements such as music and food, designed to reflect and celebrate the diversity of Kent. This allowed for an authentic representation of the various cultures present at the event, further promoting unity.

- **Pre-Event and Post-Event Engagement**: Pre-event communication highlighted the theme of cultural inclusivity, preparing attendees for a night of celebration and connection. Post-event follow-ups tracked how these interactions evolved, ensuring that initial engagements led to future collaborations.

Outcomes

The **Empower Gala** exceeded expectations in creating an inclusive, celebratory and engaging atmosphere:

- **High-Level and Culturally Diverse Attendance**: The event attracted over 150 distinguished attendees, representing a balanced mix of leaders from the Public, Private and Charity sectors, as well as a diverse array of cultural backgrounds. This blend enriched the event's atmosphere and fostered meaningful exchanges.
- **Cultural Celebration through Fashion and Atmosphere**: The **"Fashion of Wakanda"** theme was widely embraced, creating a vibrant and inclusive environment. It encouraged creativity and cultural expression, making the event not only a celebration of achievements but also of the rich cultural diversity within Kent.
- **Strong Cross-Sector and Cross-Cultural Networking**: Attendees reported that the gala was an excellent platform for networking, with many noting that new business and partnership opportunities were initiated. The diversity of the audience also enhanced the depth and breadth of these connections.

Lessons Learned

1. **Cultural Inclusivity Enhances Engagement**: Embracing diverse cultures through the event's theme and structure fostered a deeper sense of connection and belonging among attendees.

2. **High-Level Engagement Drives Future Opportunities**: By bringing together leaders from different sectors and cultural backgrounds, the gala created an atmosphere conducive to long-term collaboration and partnerships.

3. **Tracking Cultural and Sectoral Engagement is Crucial**: Post-event follow-up ensured that the connections made across sectors and cultures translated into meaningful partnerships.

Afterword

As I conclude this book, I'm reminded of the countless steps, connections and shared experiences that have shaped my journey. Writing *'Access Granted: Mastering Strategic Meetings and Events'* has been a labour of commitment, reflection and most of all, purpose. My hope is that every page equips you with insights to elevate your approach to meetings and events - transforming them from mere gatherings to pivotal moments of connection and opportunity.

In our world where access is the foundation of influence, the strategies in this book are designed to empower you to unlock doors, forge meaningful partnerships and ultimately, create lasting impact. Whether you are a seasoned professional, a curious learner, or a leader seeking the next level of strategic engagement, I encourage you to take these principles, make them your own and use them as tools to foster growth; not only in your career but in the lives and industries you touch.

Remember, access is more than just an entry point - it's the most powerful asset we have. With it, we open pathways to transformation, collaboration and global possibilities, and with each event, each handshake and each shared vision, we contribute to a greater network of change.

Thank you for being part of this journey. Here's to your success, your connections and to the doors you'll continue to unlock.

Blessing

Printed in Great Britain
by Amazon